JOHN WIMBER & KEVIN SPRINGER

AN INTERACTIVE BIBLE STUDY FOR
INDIVIDUALS, GROUPS AND SUNDAY SCHOOLS

THE WAY TO MATURITY

How to Live in the Spirit and Grow
to Maturity as a Child of God

Regal Books
A Division of Gospel Light
Ventura, California, U.S.A.

Published by Regal Books
A Division of Gospel Light
Ventura, California, U.S.A.
Printed in U.S.A.

Regal Books is a ministry of Gospel Light, an evangelical Christian publisher dedicated to serving the local church. We believe God's vision for Gospel Light is to provide church leaders with biblical, user-friendly materials that will help them evangelize, disciple and minister to children, youth and families.

It is our prayer that this Regal Book will help you discover biblical truth for your own life and help you meet the needs of others. May God richly bless you.

For a free catalog of resources from Regal Books/Gospel Light please contact your Christian supplier or call 1-800-4-GOSPEL.

ISBN 0-8307-1579-7
© 1993 by John Wimber and Kevin Springer
All rights reserved.
Printed in U.S.A.

Rights for publishing this book in other languages are contracted by Gospel Literature International (GLINT). GLINT also provides technical help for the adaptation, translation and publishing of Bible study resources and books in scores of languages worldwide. For further information, contact GLINT, P.O. Box 4060, Ontario, CA 91761-1003, U.S.A., or the publisher.

CONTENTS

Session 1
A CHANGED LIFE   19

Session 2
THE WAY TO MATURITY   31

Session 3
KNOWING GOD'S WORD   41

Session 4
HEARING GOD'S VOICE   49

111670

Session 5
KNOWING GOD

One of Jesus' primary purposes for coming to earth was to show us a full revelation of His heavenly Father (see John 1:18) and His highest purposes for us, so that we may intimately know Him.

Session 6
INTIMACY WITH THE FATHER

Our heavenly Father is calling us to experience His love, blessing, forgiveness and discipline, as His obedient sons and daughters.

Session 7
"WHO DO YOU SAY I AM?"

Because Jesus is God, we believe He possesses the power to conquer Satan (see Hebrews 2:14), perform miracles that display His Father's glory (see John 11:4,40), conquer death (see John 10:18) and save us from our sin (see 1 Peter 3:18).

Session 8
FORGIVENESS IN CHRIST

Only God's free act of forgiveness can restore our relationships with Him. Jesus' work on the cross is that free act of forgiveness, which needs to be experienced personally by faith.

Session 9
TAKING UP OUR CROSS

Jesus Christ died on the cross for us; therefore no sacrifice is too great for us to make for Him. Sacrifice for Jesus releases His power.

A NOTE FROM JOHN WIMBER AND KEVIN SPRINGER

We recently looked up the word "disciple" in a theological dictionary, and discovered that a disciple went well beyond the normal pupil-teacher relationship. In biblical times, a disciple was a pupil who learned a different way of life from a rabbi (or teacher) with whom he lived a great portion of his life. Disciples not only thought like their teachers, they talked and walked like them, taking on their deepest thoughts and character in word and deed.

The Way to Maturity is a resource for late twentieth-century disciples of Jesus. If you want to become more like your Master, then this guide is for you. Consider the discipleship opportunities awaiting you:

• Equipping for Ministry — Jesus' method of winning the world was to equip the disciples to be just like Him, then send them out into the world to touch others. To be fully equipped, we must know what we believe, why we believe it and how to apply it in everyday life. In each session you'll look at a core truth of the Christian life with these three equipping goals in mind.

• Receiving Ministry — Before we can be effective doers of God's Word, we must allow His truth to transform our hearts. In each session you will have an opportunity to receive ministry from Jesus: encouragement, empowering, forgiveness, healing, and so on.

• Involvement in Ministry — For most Christians, the period of greatest growth comes as we pass on to others what we have learned about the Christian life. Outreach is a primary goal of all discipleship, helping others to get grounded in an eternal relationship with Christ. At the end of every session you will be challenged to put into action some key aspect of what you have learned about the Christian life.

Jesus didn't call converts, He called disciples. We challenge you to use *The Way to Maturity* as a personal road map to discipleship opportunities. If you do, your life will be changed, along with many of the lives you come into contact with!

John Wimber and Kevin Springer

WHAT YOU NEED TO KNOW ABOUT...

JOINING A GROUP THAT WILL CHANGE YOUR LIFE

PURPOSE: To grow closer to God and to lay biblical foundations in our lives for continued growth and change.

PARTICIPANTS: If you're wondering if this group is for you or someone you know, see if you fit into this list:

> ❖ **Anyone wanting to experience significant change in their lives.**
>
> ❖ **Seekers:** Those who don't know where they stand with God, but are willing to explore their relationship with Him.
>
> ❖ **Strugglers:** Those who have had a relationship with Christ but want to grow closer to Him.
>
> ❖ **New Christians:** Those who have just begun a personal relationship with Jesus.
>
> ❖ **People turned off by the church:** But who are wanting to grow closer to God.

THE BIBLE: What if you don't know anything about the Bible? No problem. This study is for you. The study notes, questions and guided readings are easy to follow and designed to introduce you to the most fascinating book ever written. This study is based on the *New International Version*® (*NIV*®) translation of the Bible, but we recommend that you refer to different translations to gain a broader understanding of the passages you will study.

STUDY NOTES: Notes on the passages studied are provided in order to help you understand the passages' contexts and unfamiliar words that may need to be defined.

DIGGING DEEPER: For more background on topics discussed in this study, read John Wimber and Kevin Springer's book, *Power Points* (San Francisco: HarperCollins, 1991).

DISCUSS: We will discuss how we can understand and live out truths from Scripture on growing close to God.

COMMITMENT: The group is designed to last 13 sessions, with each session building on the previous ones. For maximum growth, make regular attendance a high priority.

EXTENDED STUDY: Scripture reading and follow-up questions will help you integrate into your daily experience what you learn and help you prepare for the next session. The time and effort you put into this study will determine the quality and depth of the next session.

KEY VERSE: Each session has a key verse that captures the essence of a growing relationship with God. You will benefit greatly from memorizing it. There are three secrets to memorizing Scripture: (1) Review it; (2) Review it; (3) Review it.

GROUP GUIDELINES: Groups run better when they follow these rules:

❖ In a spiritual growth group there is no such thing as asking a stupid question or making a dumb remark. We're all learners and learners can only grow through trial and error.

❖ Be respectful of other members in the group, allowing opportunity for everyone to contribute. Everyone should be able to participate and no one should be allowed to dominate.

❖ If you have not been able to prepare for a session, work at being a good listener.

❖ All *personal* information heard in the group should remain in the group. Don't repeat what you've heard to people outside the group.

WHAT YOU NEED TO KNOW ABOUT...

LEADING AN INTERACTIVE BIBLE STUDY

OPTIONS: *The Way to Maturity* may be used in a variety of settings: Sunday School, midweek small-group gatherings, weekend retreats, or on your own. You may use all 13 sessions, an abbreviated eight-session format, or a five-session retreat format.

LENGTH: Optional discussion questions allow for flexibility in the length of the study—from 60 to 90 minutes.

GROUP SIZE: The best size for a spiritual growth group is between 12 to 20—small enough for meaningful fellowship, but large enough for dynamic group interaction.

NEW MEMBERS: You may decide to encourage members to invite a friend to the study. After the third session we suggest you stop opening up the group to new members.

TIPS FOR GUIDING GROUP INTERACTION

Many adults resist participating in groups that feature interaction—and with good reason. Discussions can and often do encounter the following problems:

❖ Rabbit trails—somehow things can get off track;

❖ Pooling ignorance—group members have opinions and feelings without having any solid knowledge of the topic;

❖ Filibuster—a group member talks so much or so often that others are intimidated into nonparticipation (see shrinking violet);

- ◆ Discomfort zone—group members are expected to talk about matters that make them feel awkward (see shrinking violet);

- ◆ Shrinking violet—a group member is intimidated into silence;

- ◆ Flying fur—opening up for comments from individuals may result in disagreements being aired;

- ◆ Popularity poll—issues may end up being resolved by majority opinion rather than knowledgeable grounds.

In spite of all these, as well as other pitfalls, getting a group of adults actively involved in discussing issues of the Christian life is highly worthwhile. Not only does group interaction help to create interest, stimulate thinking and encourage effective learning, it is vital for building quality relationships within the group. Only as people begin to share their thoughts and feelings do they begin to build bonds of friendship and support.

Granted, some people prefer to bypass any group participation and get right to the content ("I just want to study [or listen to Dr. Smith teach] the Bible—I don't have time to get to know a bunch of strangers."). However, it has never been possible to effectively separate knowledge and love. Truth apart from touch will turn to untruth. While group interaction may at times seem difficult and even nonproductive, leaders and group members can work together to achieve positive results.

The following tips are helpful in making group interaction a positive learning opportunity for everyone, helping to build a climate of loving acceptance and openness to growth:

- ◆ When a question or comment is raised that is off the subject, either suggest that it be dealt with at another time, or ask the group if they would prefer to pursue the new issue now.

❖ When someone talks too much, direct a few questions specifically to other people, making sure not to put a shy person on the spot. Talk privately with the dominating person, asking for cooperation in helping to draw out a few of the quieter group members.

❖ When someone does not participate verbally, assign a few questions to be discussed in pairs, trios or other small groups. Or, invite people to write their answer to a specific question or two. Then invite several people (including the quiet person) to read what they wrote.

❖ If someone asks a question to which you do not know the answer, admit it and move on. If the question calls for insight about personal experience, invite group members to comment. If the question requires specialized knowledge, offer to look for an answer (in the library, from your pastor, etc.) before the next session.

❖ When group members disagree with you or each other, remind the group that it is possible to disagree without becoming disagreeable. To help clarify the issues while maintaining a climate of mutual acceptance, try one or two of these approaches:

❖ Encourage those on opposite sides to restate what they have heard the other person(s) say about the issue. Then invite each side to evaluate how accurately they feel their positions were presented.

❖ Ask group members to identify as many points as possible related to the topic on which both sides agree.

❖ Lead the group in examining Scripture passages related to the topic, looking for common ground that they can all accept.

❖ Urge group members to keep an open heart and mind and a willingness to continue loving one another, while learning more about the topic at hand.

If the disagreement involves an issue on which your church has stated a position, be sure that stance is clearly and positively presented. This should be done not to squelch dissent, but to ensure there is no confusion over where your church stands.

THE WAY TO MATURITY–COURSE OVERVIEW

"Ask where the good way is, and walk in it,
and you will find rest for your souls."
Jeremiah 6:16

THE SESSIONS AT A GLANCE

A CHANGED LIFE

This life was not intended to be the place of our perfection but the preparation for it.

Richard Baxter, author and pastor,

1615–91

SESSION FOCUS
Spiritual growth is a lifelong process of growing closer to God that begins with a person-to-person relationship with Jesus.

SESSION KEYS

KEY VERSE (Commit it to memory.)
[Christ said,] "For God so loved the world that he gave his one and only Son, that whoever believes in him shall not perish but have eternal life." John 3:16

KEY RESOURCES

A.W. Tozer's *That Incredible Christian* (Camp Hill: Christian Publications, 1986), pages 11-19; Dallas Willard's *The Spirit of the Disciplines* (San Francisco: HarperCollins, 1988), chapters 1-3; and John Wimber and Kevin Springer's *Power Points* (San Francisco: HarperCollins, 1991).

SESSION 1 AT A GLANCE

Section	60 Minutes	90 Minutes	What You'll Do
Orientation	5	5	Review Group Guidelines
Openers	10	15	Answer and Discuss Questions
Thinking It Through	25	40	Discuss the Meaning of Key Scriptures for Spiritual Growth: John 3:16-18; Philippians 3:12-16
Working It Out	10	20	Draw Conclusions and Make Life Applications
Looking Ahead	5	5	Preparation for Next Session
Wrapping Up	5	5	Close with Prayer or Song

Leader's Tip: *Carefully consider the purpose of your group and provide ground rules that will advance that purpose.*

ORIENTATION
Take 5 minutes for both sessions

After opening in prayer, take five minutes to review the approach to each session and the overall direction of the study, including expectations for preparation, visitors, etc. Refer back to the "Charting Your Change" and "Joining a Group that Will Change Your Life" sections in the introductory pages.

Break up into groups of three to five people.

The first question is for groups who don't know each other well. If you know each other, start with question 2.

OPENERS
Take 10 minutes for 60-minute session
Take 15 minutes for 90-minute session

The following questions help you to better know other members of the group and will introduce you to many of the topics that we will cover over the next 13 sessions. Share your responses with the group.

1. Share your answers with the group to the following questions:
   • Where were you living when you were 10 years old?

   • At age 10, how many brothers and sisters did you have and how old were they?

   • Could you describe a place, person, or time that was a source of warmth for you at age 10?

The remaining questions in this section are designed to get you into this session's topic.

2. Which of the following terms describe your current relationship with God? Why? (You may ✔ one or two.)

___ Distant	___ Intimate
___ Forgiving	___ Shaky
___ Silent	___ Loving
___ Growing	___ Plateaued
___ Fearful	___ Open
___ Healing	___ Confusing
___ Disappointing	___ Frustrating

3. Who carries most of the responsibility for your spiritual growth—you or God?

OPTIONAL QUESTIONS FOR 90-MINUTE SESSION

4. Have you ever had an extended period of time in which you felt close to God and as a result your life was changed in a significant way? Describe your relationship with God during that time and why you think it stopped growing.

5. What comes to mind when you hear the term "spiritual growth"?

6. How would you summarize your thoughts on how we grow closer to God?

7. Are you satisfied with your spiritual growth since becoming a Christian?

Bring the whole group back together; the leader should take two to three minutes to introduce this section.

***Leader's Tip:** Take three to four minutes to share some aspect of your spiritual growth.*

THINKING IT THROUGH
Take 25 minutes for 60-minute session
Take 40 minutes for 90-minute session

What do you think of when you hear terms like "spiritual growth," "mature faith," and "growing closer to God"? Many of us struggle with vague feelings of guilt, of falling short of some indefinite or uncertain standard. Sources of that standard may differ for each of us: parents, educators, peers, the media, our conscience and so on. People who are seeking God are aware of an even higher standard for growth and maturity that is found in the Bible.

Frequently we struggle with guilt and discouragement because, no matter how hard we try, we can't measure up to God's standards. We always seem to fall short of the righteousness and love of God, even when we give our best shots at following good rules, obeying sure principles and conforming to high moral standards of behavior.

But is this kind of frustrating (and impossible!) effort truly the essence of growth and change? Over the course of this study we'll learn that God's ways are different from the world's ways and that they are much more rewarding.

In this session and the next we'll look at a few passages of Scripture that capture the meaning of growth in Christ. As an individual, you'll evaluate where in the growth process you are. And we'll learn that spiritual maturity is an obtainable and reasonable goal.

Now return to your small groups to read the passage and discuss the questions.

TRUE CHANGE BEGINS WITH KNOWING JESUS

Read Jesus' teaching in John 3:16-18. Answer the following questions and discuss your responses with your group.

This passage is foundational for new Christians to understand.

1. In verse 16, who did Jesus claim to be and what did He come into the world to do?

Leader's Tip: Ask someone in the group to read the entire passage aloud, then give the group a minute or two to review the questions for a guided discussion.

2. What do we have to do to enter into a relationship with Jesus?

3. What are some characteristics of eternal life? When does it begin?

OPTIONAL QUESTIONS FOR 90-MINUTE SESSION

4. What does Jesus say about condemnation?

5. Why did Jesus need to take the initiative for us to have eternal life? (Hint: see John 3:3.)

SCRIPTURE NOTES

John's Gospel is "written that you may believe that Jesus is the Christ, the Son of God and that by believing you may have life in his name" (John 20:31). In other words, John's primary purpose in writing was evangelistic, to spread the good news that Jesus died on the cross and through faith in Him we have eternal life.

Jesus' words in John 3:16-18 are part of a much larger dialogue He is having with a Jewish leader by the name of Nicodemus. Nicodemus was trying to figure out who Jesus was and how Jesus could perform miraculous signs and—most importantly—how to enter the Kingdom of God. Jesus responded with a hard saying, "No one can see the kingdom of God unless he is born again [or, born from above]" (John 3:3). John 3:16-18 is found at the very heart of Jesus' response and it summarizes the essence of the gospel, of what it means to be born again: God initiates our salvation; it is motivated by His love; our salvation cost God His own Son's life on the cross; all that God requires of us for salvation is faith in His Son; in salvation we receive eternal life (a new quality of life) and we are freed from condemnation.

CHANGE IS A LIFELONG PROCESS

Read Philippians 3:12-16. As a group, answer the questions that follow and discuss your responses.

1. What does the author mean when he said he hasn't yet "been made perfect" in verse 12? (Hint: see Ephesians 4:11-13.)

2. In Philippians 3:14, what goal do you think the author is referring to? (Hint: see Philippians 3:8-10.)

3. When do you believe the author thinks we reach perfection? Does this encourage or discourage you?

OPTIONAL QUESTIONS FOR 90-MINUTE SESSION

4. Using the word picture of a race, how does the author describe our part in this lifelong process?

5. According to Philippians 3:15, how should mature Christians view those who are less mature?

SCRIPTURE NOTES

Earlier in Philippians 3, the apostle Paul is warning his readers about opponents (he refers to them as "dogs"!) who are "mutilators of the flesh" (Philippians 3:2). These people, called Judaizers in Paul's letter to the Galatians, were teaching the necessity of works to be saved (in this case, circumcision). Paul strongly objected, arguing that we are saved only by placing our faith in the finished work of Jesus Christ: "I want to know Christ and the power of his resurrection and the fellowship of sharing in his sufferings, becoming like him in his death, and so, somehow, to attain to the resurrection from the dead" (Philippians 3:10,11). Then, to clarify his thought, Paul states clearly that the conclusion must not be drawn that he (or any of us) has already reached the state of perfection in our faith (see Philippians 3:12-16).

A special note on "perfection." Perfection is Paul's goal and as long as he is on earth he will strive to reach that goal (Philippians 3:14). But what does Paul mean by perfection? The person who has "been made perfect" (Philippians 3:12) is fully grown, mature, complete, adult—not flawlessly perfect. Perfection describes a quality relationship with God, one marked by habitual intimacy and dependence on His grace. In fact, the Greek word translated "perfect" in Philippians 3:12 is translated "mature" in Philippians 3:15. The mature person, then, is one who has made reasonable progress in his or her spiritual growth (see Philippians 3:15).

Remain in your small groups for this section.

Leader's Tip: *For the 60-minute session, you will have time to answer only one question.*

WORKING IT OUT

Take 10 minutes for 60-minute session
Take 20 minutes for 90-minute session

1. How does Paul's perspective on spiritual growth (i.e., that growth is a lifelong process) help me to better understand the ups and downs of my relationship with God?

2. What single aspect of spiritual growth that we have discussed in this session stands out in my mind? Why?

3. What concrete steps can I take this week to begin growing closer to God?

Bring the whole group back together for this section.

Leader's Tip:
Encourage the group to take several days to reflect on and pray daily about this session, asking God to show them what areas of their lives they need to change in light of what they have learned.

LOOKING AHEAD

Take 5 minutes for both sessions

NEXT SESSION: THE WAY TO MATURITY

Without a clear vision of what God is transforming us into, we remain unsure about our progress. We'll take a closer look at the path and goal of spiritual growth.

To get acquainted with the way to maturity, follow the daily Scripture readings on the next page.

DAILY SCRIPTURE READINGS

Day	Text	Challenge Question
Reflection on This Session		
1	1 Corinthians 9:24-27	What motivates Paul to keep running the race of the Christian life?
2	1 Corinthians 12:31b—13:13	According to Paul, what should be our motivation for living the Christian life?
3	Romans 8:1-17	Write down the advantages of living by the Spirit over living by the law.
Looking Ahead		
4	John 8:31-41	What relationship does Jesus see between our belief and our behavior?
5	Matthew 6:1-18	What is Jesus most concerned about as we give, pray and fast?

In preparation, look at next session's Scripture Notes. Be ready to share your responses to the questions with the rest of the group. Finally, start to memorize the key verses for the next session—Galatians 5:22-23:

But the fruit of the Spirit is love, joy, peace, patience, kindness, goodness, faithfulness, gentleness and self-control. Against such things there is no law.

THE WAY TO MATURITY

$\mathcal{S}$piritual growth consists most in the growth of the root, which is out of sight.

Matthew Henry, pastor and Bible commentator, 1662 –1714

SESSION FOCUS

Spiritual growth arises from our sincere, active cooperation with the initiating, empowering work of the Holy Spirit and results in habits of righteousness.

SESSION KEYS

KEY VERSES (Commit them to memory.)
"But the fruit of the Spirit is love, joy, peace, patience, kindness, goodness, faithfulness, gentleness and self-control. Against such things there is no law." Galatians 5:22,23

KEY RESOURCES

A.W. Tozer's *That Incredible Christian* (Camp Hill: Christian Publications, 1986), pages 20-34; David Watson's *Called and Committed* (Wheaton: Harold Shaw Publishing, 1982); Dallas Willard's *The Spirit of the Disciplines* (San Francisco: HarperCollins, 1988), chapters 4,5; and John Wimber and Kevin Springer's *Power Points* (San Francisco: HarperCollins, 1991), chapter 2.

SESSION 2 AT A GLANCE

Section	60 Minutes	90 Minutes	What You'll Do
Getting Started	5	5	Pray and Worship
Openers	10	15	Answer and Discuss Questions
Thinking It Through	25	40	Discuss the Meaning of Key Scriptures on How We Grow: John 8:27-41; Matthew 6:1-18
Working It Out	10	20	Draw Conclusions and Make Life Applications
Looking Ahead	5	5	Preparation for Next Session
Wrapping Up	5	5	Close with Prayer or Song

Break up into groups of
three to five people.

OPENERS

Take 10 minutes for 60-minute session
Take 15 minutes for 90-minute session

1. When you see the word "obedience" in the Bible, is your initial reaction more positive or negative? More "What a fantastic opportunity" or "Oh no, another limitation"?

2. Choose one word to describe your motivation for obeying God and explain why you chose that word. (You are not limited to the following list.)

Fear	Love
Intimacy	Acceptance
Joy	Rejection
Performance	Unsure
What others think	Rewards

OPTIONAL QUESTIONS FOR
90-MINUTE SESSION

On a scale of 1 to 10, with 1 indicating low agreement and 10 high agreement, circle the number that corresponds to your belief or experience:

Low					Level of Agreement			High		Statement
1	2	3	4	5	6	7	8	9	10	I have a clear, biblical understanding of personal prayer.
1	2	3	4	5	6	7	8	9	10	I am basically satisfied with my personal prayer life.
1	2	3	4	5	6	7	8	9	10	I am satisfied with my motives for personal prayer.
1	2	3	4	5	6	7	8	9	10	I have a clear, biblical understanding of why we are supposed to fast.
1	2	3	4	5	6	7	8	9	10	When I read Scripture I think about how it affects my life-style.
1	2	3	4	5	6	7	8	9	10	I have a clear, biblical understanding of financial giving to the Lord's work.
1	2	3	4	5	6	7	8	9	10	The way I handle money conforms to what the Bible teaches on stewardship.
1	2	3	4	5	6	7	8	9	10	I am satisfied with my motivation for financial giving.

Share your lowest and highest agreement levels to the above statements with the group, offering reasons for your answers.

Bring the whole group back together and the leader should take two to three minutes to introduce this section.

THINKING IT THROUGH

Take 25 minutes for 60-minute session
Take 40 minutes for 90-minute session

Though Christians believe that God's Word is our unchanging standard, we still frequently stumble into traps set through the false belief systems of the world. Here are two traps that this lesson deals with:

First, there is intellectualism, the seeking of academic knowledge for knowledge's sake. Christians fall into this trap when they "know" biblical truth but fail to practice it. In Matthew 23:1-11 Jesus tells the multitudes that the theology of the religious leaders is fine, but their deeds are inconsistent with their words. In other words, the religious leaders "know" but they don't act on what they know. Why? Because they are looking for the approval of men rather than of God (see verse 5).

The antidote for intellectualism is simple: there is no true "knowing" without doing (see John 8:27-41).

Second, there is outward obedience, the outward conformity to high ethical, moral and biblical standards as a means to maturity. We do believe that disciplines like generosity, prayer, Bible study and fasting produce growth, if we are actively cooperating from our hearts with the work of the Holy Spirit. Though God is vitally concerned with obedience, He is more concerned with what motivates us. This is a matter of the heart, of the core of our being.

In Matthew 21:28-32, Jesus rebukes the religious leaders who, by all outward appearances, conformed to the Old Testament law. He told them that the "tax collectors and the prostitutes are entering the kingdom of God ahead of you" (Matthew 21:31). Outward conformity to a set of laws is not enough, because—after hearing the truth—"you did not repent and believe him" (Matthew 21:32).

The antidote for outward obedience is to develop a secret history with the Father (see Matthew 6:1-18).

When we believe from the heart, we will obey. This is the kind of obedience that pleases God and produces the fruit of the Spirit.

Now return to your small groups to read the passage and discuss the questions.

CHANGE IS A LIFELONG PROCESS THAT INVOLVES ENCOUNTERING, BELIEVING, AND OBEYING GOD'S TRUTH

Read John 8:27-41. Answer the questions that follow and discuss your responses with your group. Note Jesus' repeated use of family words (father, children, descendants) with behavioral words (do, doing).

1. What relationship does Jesus see between spiritual ancestry and behavior (verses 28,29,39,40)?

2. What kind of "knowing" the truth does Jesus say sets us free (verses 31,32)? How does this differ from the modern, academic sense of "knowing"?

3. From what does the truth set us free (verses 33,34)?

4. How does Jesus set an example of obedience for us (verses 28,29)?

SCRIPTURE NOTES

In John 8:31-32 Jesus is addressing Jews who made formal declarations of faith in Him, but who were probably not true believers (see John 8:33, 37). We do what we hear from our Father (see John 8:38), because we know our loving Father always has our best interest at heart. Relationship influences motives. What differentiates false belief from true belief is what follows: obedience from a heart that loves God. If we truly hear and know the truth, then we will believe and act on it. It is the truth that we both know and do that frees us from bondage to sin.

OPTIONAL PASSAGE FOR 90-MINUTE SESSION

HABITS OF RIGHTEOUSNESS ARE MORE CONCERNED WITH OUR CHARACTER THAN WITH CONFORMITY TO EXTERNAL STANDARDS

Read Jesus' teaching in Matthew 6:1-18. As a group, answer the following questions and discuss your responses.

1. What motivation does Jesus warn the disciples to avoid when they give, pray and fast (verse 1)? Do you ever struggle with this motivation?

2. What will be our reward if we are improperly motivated (verses 2,5,16)?

3. According to Jesus, what should our motivation be for giving, praying and fasting? What will then be our reward (verses 3,4,6,17,18)?

4. Read the Lord's Prayer to yourself (verses 9-13). What one word can you think of to describe the quality of relationship Jesus had with His heavenly Father? Does your prayer life exhibit any of these qualities?

5. Twelve of Jesus' 38 parables had to do with money. Why do you think Jesus placed such an emphasis on giving?

6. Have you ever tried fasting (verses 16-18)? What do you think of the idea of fasting?

SCRIPTURE NOTES

The Gospel of Matthew was written by Matthew, 1 of the 12 apostles. He was a tax collector who walked away from his work to follow Jesus (see Matthew 9:9-13). He wrote his Gospel to convince Jews that Jesus was the promised Messiah. He frequently quotes from the Old Testament to demonstrate that Jesus fulfilled predictions concerning the Messiah.

In Matthew 6:1-18, which is part of a larger discourse called the Sermon on the Mount, Jesus is commenting to His disciples on what the Jews considered the three cardinal works of the religious life—giving, praying and fasting. He doesn't dispute their importance, though He does question their value if done for the wrong motives. For Jesus, external conformity to high standards is of no benefit unless accompanied by humility, dependence on God and, above all else, a desire to please the Father.

Remain in your small groups for this section.

Leader's Tip: *For the 60-minute session, you will have time to answer only one question.*

WORKING IT OUT

Take 10 minutes for 60-minute session
Take 20 minutes for 90-minute session

1. Is God speaking to you through His Word about an area of your life that He wants to change, so that it is more conformed to His Word? Share the area with the group and have them pray for you, asking the Holy Spirit to give you wisdom and power for change from the inside out.

2. What concrete steps can you take this week to improve your practice in this area of your life or in one of the three areas discussed in Matthew—giving, praying and fasting?

Bring the whole group back together for this section.

Leader's Tip:
Encourage the group to take several days to reflect on and pray daily about this session, asking God to show them what areas of their lives they need to change in light of what they have learned.

LOOKING AHEAD

Take 5 minutes for both sessions

NEXT SESSION: KNOWING GOD'S WORD

Spiritual growth involves walking a well-trod path. But how can we know for sure that we are on the right path? There are many "voices" and "gods" calling us to their paths, but they all lead to darkness and death.

The way to the Lord is illumined by His Word, through which He reveals Himself in all of His splendor. In the next session we'll look at how Scripture satisfies our thirst for God, for it leads us to a full relationship with Jesus.

To reinforce what you've learned this session and prepare for the next session, follow these daily Scripture readings:

DAILY SCRIPTURE READINGS

Day	Text	Challenge Question
Reflection on This Session		
1	Psalm 119:1-8,57-64	What does the psalmist say about obedience?
2	Psalm 119:65-72,100-112	Why is obedience important?
3	Psalm 119:89-104	What benefits do we have from God's Word?
Looking Ahead		
4	Matthew 4:1-11	What is the primary weapon that Jesus chose to resist Satan's attacks?
5	2 Timothy 3:14-17	If you are truly submitting to Scripture, what can it accomplish in your life (verses 16,17)?

In preparation, look at next session's Scripture Notes. Be ready to share your responses to the questions with the rest of the group. Finally, start to memorize the key verses for the next session—2 Timothy 3:16,17:

All Scripture is God-breathed and is useful for teaching, rebuking, correcting and training in righteousness, so that the man of God may be thoroughly equipped for every good work.

KNOWING GOD'S WORD

The Scriptures were not given to increase our knowledge but to change our lives.

D. L. Moody, evangelist,
1837-99

SESSION FOCUS
God reveals Himself through His Word, the Bible. When we submit to the Bible, our lives are changed and empowered.

SESSION KEYS

KEY VERSES (Commit them to memory.)
"All Scripture is God-breathed and is useful for teaching, rebuking, correcting and training in righteousness, so that the man of God may be thoroughly equipped for every good work." 2 Timothy 3:16,17

KEY RESOURCES

David Watson's *Called and Committed* (Wheaton: Harold Shaw Publishing, 1982), chapter 7; and John Wimber and Kevin Springer's *Power Points* (San Francisco: HarperCollins, 1991), chapters 3-7.

SESSION 3 AT A GLANCE

Section	60 Minutes	90 Minutes	What You'll Do
Getting Started	5	5	Pray and Worship
Openers	10	15	Answer and Discuss Questions
Thinking It Through	25	40	Discuss the Meaning of Key Scriptures for Knowing God's Word: 2 Timothy 3:14-17; Matthew 4:1-11
Working It Out	10	20	Draw Conclusions and Make Life Applications
Looking Ahead	5	5	Preparation for Next Session
Wrapping Up	5	5	Close with Prayer or Song

Break up into groups of three to five people.

Leader's Tip: The purpose of these questions is to help understand the power of the written word.

OPENERS

Take 10 minutes for 60-minute session
Take 15 minutes for 90-minute session

1. Name one or two books (or book series)—other than the Bible—that have greatly influenced you at different times in your life.

2. How old were you when you read them and how did they affect your life?

3. What are the primary reasons that motivate you to read Scripture?

____ To follow along with the Sunday sermon.
____ A desire to learn about God.
____ A desire to grow closer to God.
____ Because I've always heard that I need to in order to grow.
____ Obedience, but I get discouraged easily.
____ To find justification for what I'm doing.
____ I feel guilty when I don't.
____ I don't read the Bible that often, because I'm not sure why I should.
____ A desire to know God more personally
____ Other _____

OPTIONAL QUESTIONS FOR 90-MINUTE SESSION

4. At any time in your life, has God spoken to you through any of the following means?
  a. The creation.
  b. Your conscience.
  c. Life's circumstances.
  d. Other sources.

5. What kind of knowledge did you gain from these sources?

6. How is the knowledge of God gained from Scripture different from that gained from other sources?

*Bring the whole group
back together and the
leader should take two to
three minutes to intro-
duce this section.*

THINKING IT THROUGH

Take 25 minutes for 60-minute session
Take 40 minutes for 90-minute session

Jesus believed the Bible was the Word of God. First, He thought that it was the final authority in matters of truth and ethics. During one controversy with religious leaders He said, "the Scripture cannot be broken" (John 10:35) and He rooted the authority for His teaching in God's word (see Mark 7:6-13).

Jesus also held and taught an exceedingly high view of Scripture. In Matthew 5:17 He said, "Do not think that I have come to abolish the Law or the Prophets; I have not come to abolish them but to fulfill them."

If Jesus believed the Bible was God's Word and taught that we should obey it, then we shouldn't be surprised to discover that the Bible is food for growth and a light for the path that we walk.

*Now return to your small
groups to read the pas-
sage and discuss the
questions.*

GOD'S ACTIVE INVOLVEMENT IN THE WRITING OF SCRIPTURE IS SO PERVASIVE AND POWERFUL THAT, AS WE SUBMIT TO IT, OUR LIVES WILL BE TRANSFORMED

Read 2 Timothy 3:14-17. As a group, answer the following questions and discuss your responses.

1. In verse 14 Paul is referring to himself as well as Timothy's mother and grandmother (see 2 Timothy 1:5). Based on this, how important is good biblical instruction to spiritual growth? What sort of things do you think Timothy had become "convinced of"? (Hint: see 2 Timothy 1:8-12.)

2. What does Paul mean by "God-breathed" when he refers to Scripture? (Hint: see 2 Peter 1:19-21.) Have you ever had an experience while reading Scripture that illustrated its divine origin?

3. According to 2 Timothy 3:16, all Scripture is useful for "teaching, rebuking, correcting and training." Can you tell of a time when Scripture accomplished one of these in you?

4. In what sense does Paul speak of us being "thoroughly equipped for every good work" in verse 17? Give an illustration of how Scripture has equipped you for a good work.

Scripture Notes provide a simple background to the texts. The leader should review the notes ahead of the study and be prepared to summarize them for the group.

SCRIPTURE NOTES

Second Timothy was written by Paul when he was imprisoned in Rome. It is a "pastoral letter" to his young assistant, Timothy, who was overseeing the church in Ephesus. Paul wrote the letter around A.D. 66-67, about 40 years after the death and resurrection of Christ.

In 2 Timothy 3:14-17, Paul appeals to Timothy to remain loyal to the basics of the faith, those truths that are rooted in Scripture. Scripture brings salvation, instructs, corrects, finds fault (for the sake of correction), trains in the right thing to do—in summary, it is nothing less than the source of guidance in how we can know and serve God. Any Christian, but especially leaders, must root their lives in the Bible, seeking to know and live what it teaches.

OPTIONAL QUESTIONS FOR
90-MINUTE SESSION

Leader's Tip: Bring the larger group back together and take four or five minutes and allow different members of the group to share about what they learned from 2 Timothy 3.

Now return to your small groups.

THE WORD OF GOD PROVIDES POWER FOR RESISTING TEMPTATION

Read Jesus' teaching in Matthew 4:1-11. As a group, answer the following questions and discuss your responses.

1. What is the primary weapon Jesus used to resist Satan's attacks (verses 4,7,10)? (Hint: see Ephesians 6:17.)

2. In Matthew 4:4, Jesus refers to living "on every word that comes from the mouth of God." How can we do this? (Hint: see Deuteronomy 8:3)

3. Do you believe there is any temptation or test that Scripture would not equip you to resist? Have you ever had an experience in which you used Scripture to resist a temptation to sin? Describe it. (See 1 Corinthians 10:13. Scripture can be a means of escape from temptation. Jesus uses it this way in Matthew 4:1-11.)

SCRIPTURE NOTES

In Matthew 4:1-11 Jesus is led by the Spirit into the wilderness to be tested. This happened just prior to His public ministry and the satanic attacks never let up throughout the remainder of His life (see Mark 8:33;

Luke 4:13). Throughout His ministry, Jesus never wavered from His strategy of spiritual warfare: whenever Satan attacked, Jesus resisted him with God's Word. Jesus refused to rely on His supernatural power or to compromise; He responded to every temptation with total reliance on His Father's word, as embodied in Scripture.

Remain in your small groups for this section.

Leader's Tip: For the 60-minute session, you will have time to answer only one question.

WORKING IT OUT

Take 10 minutes for 60-minute session
Take 20 minutes for 90-minute session

1. How has this session altered your view of Scripture?

2. How much time do you believe a Christian should spend reading the Bible?

3. If you had held a personal opinion about something for a long time and then discovered a passage in the Bible that contradicted it, what would you do?

Bring the whole group back together for this section.

Leader's Tip: Encourage the group to take several days to reflect on and pray daily about this session, asking God to show them what areas of their lives they need to change in light of what they have learned.

LOOKING AHEAD

Take 5 minutes for both sessions

NEXT SESSION: HEARING GOD'S VOICE

David Watson, in his book *Called and Committed*, says, "If every word that God speaks is vital for us, how does God speak today? How can we both hear and understand His word rightly?" Next session we'll explore how to interpret the Bible and how God speaks through other means—such as dreams and visions, inner impressions and so on.

To reinforce what you've learned this session and pre-pare for the next session, follow these daily Scripture readings:

DAILY SCRIPTURE READINGS

Day	Text	Challenge Question
Reflection on This Session		
1	1 Peter 1:22—2:3	Peter says to "crave pure spiritual milk" in 2:2. What is the spiritual milk to which he refers (1 Peter 1:23,25)?
2	Hebrews 4:12,13	What ways does God's Word penetrate our hearts?
3	Matthew 5:17-20	In what sense does Jesus mean our righteousness must surpass that of the law (verse 20)?
Looking Ahead		
4	Luke 12:1-12	How does the Holy Spirit speak to us when we are in need of God's guidance?
5	1 Samuel 3:1—4:1	Do you believe God can speak to you today in a fashion similar to how He spoke to Samuel?

In preparation, look at next session's Scripture Notes. Be ready to share your responses to the questions with the rest of the group. Finally, start to memorize the key verse for the next session—John 10:27:

[Jesus said,] "My sheep listen to my voice; I know them, and they follow me."

HEARING GOD'S VOICE

Do not leave my cry unanswered. Whisper words of truth in my heart, for you alone speak truth.

Saint Augustine, Bishop of Hippo in North Africa, 354 –430

SESSION FOCUS
The Bible clearly teaches that God delights to communicate with His people. We should expect Him to speak to us in a variety of ways and learn to hear His voice.

SESSION KEYS

KEY VERSE (Commit it to memory.)
[Jesus said,] "My sheep listen to my voice; I know them and they follow me." John 10:27

KEY RESOURCES

Klaus Bockmuehl's *Listening to the God Who Speaks* (Colorado Springs: Helmers and Howard Publications, 1990); Joyce Huggett's *The Joy of Listening to God* (Downer's Grove: InterVarsity Press, 1987); David Watson's *Called and Committed* (Wheaton: Harold Shaw Publishing, 1982), chapter 7; and John Wimber and Kevin Springer's *Power Points* (San Francisco: HarperCollins, 1991), chapters 8-10.

SESSION 4 AT A GLANCE

Section	60 Minutes	90 Minutes	What You'll Do
Getting Started	5	5	Pray and Worship
Openers	10	15	Answer and Discuss Questions
Thinking It Through	25	40	Discuss the Meaning of Key Scriptures for Hearing God's Voice: 1 Samuel 3:1—4:1; Acts 8:26-40
Working It Out	10	20	Draw Conclusions and Make Life Applications
Looking Ahead	5	5	Preparation for Next Session
Wrapping Up	5	5	Close with Prayer or Song

Break up into groups of three to five people.

OPENERS

Take 10 minutes for 60-minute session
Take 15 minutes for 90-minute session

1. "I believe God still speaks to Christians today through means other than the Bible." Why do you agree or disagree with this statement?

2. Have you ever had an experience in which you sensed God was speaking to you? Describe the experience. Did you act on what you heard?

OPTIONAL QUESTION FOR 90-MINUTE SESSION

3. Have you ever experienced what you believed was a dream or vision from God? What criteria did you use to evaluate if it was actually from God or from another source?

Bring the whole group back together and the leader should take two to three minutes to introduce this section.

THINKING IT THROUGH

Take 25 minutes for 60-minute session
Take 40 minutes for 90-minute session

Scripture is full of admonitions to listen to God. For example, at the Transfiguration (see Matthew 17:1-5), God commanded the disciples to listen to Jesus.

The Old Testament prophets frequently told the people to listen (see Jeremiah 7:2; 30:2; Ezekiel 37:4) and the book of Revelation calls the churches to "hear what the Spirit says" (see Revelation 2:7,11,17,29; 3:6). As Frank Buchman writes, "When man listens, God speaks. When man obeys, God acts....We are not out to tell God. We are out to let God tell us....The lesson the world most needs is the art of listening to God."

Jesus asserted that hearing His voice was prerequisite to being an obedient disciple. He said, "My sheep listen to my voice; I know them and they follow me" (John 10:27). But how do we hear His voice? Last session we saw that the primary place to hear God is in His Word, the Bible. The Bible itself teaches that God speaks to His people in other ways; not only through the preaching, teaching and study of the Word, but also through dreams and visions, circumstances, angels, inner impressions and so on. In the remainder of this session we'll look at a few of those ways.

Now return to your small groups to read the passage and discuss the questions.

GOD DELIGHTS IN SPEAKING TO US, BUT WE MUST LEARN TO RECOGNIZE HIS VOICE

Read 1 Samuel 3:1—4:1. As a group, answer the questions that follow and discuss your responses.

1. Why were Eli and Samuel so slow to recognize the Lord was speaking (1 Samuel 3:1)?

2. Why do you think there was such little revelation at this time? (Hint: see 1 Samuel 2:22-26; Amos 8:11-12.)

3. Who initiated the communication (1 Samuel:3:4,6,8)?

4. What was Samuel's basic heart attitude (1 Samuel 3:5,6,8,10)?

5. What did Samuel recognize his experience to be (1 Samuel 3:10,15)?

6. What is the relationship between knowing God and hearing His voice (1 Samuel 3:7)?

7. How could you sum up this passage in respect to hearing God's voice?

OPTIONAL QUESTION FOR 90-MINUTE SESSION

8. Where was Samuel sleeping when God spoke to him (1 Samuel 3:3)? What does this teach you about where we can hear the voice of God?

Scripture Notes provide a simple background to the texts. The leader should review the notes ahead of the study and be prepared to summarize them for the group.

SCRIPTURE NOTES

First and 2 Samuel are named after the prophet Samuel, who anointed both Saul and David, Israel's first kings. Originally 1 and 2 Samuel were one book, but were divided into two books in the third century B.C. First and 2 Samuel record the establishment of kingship in Israel, focusing on the lives of Samuel, Saul and David. These events covered the years 1105 to 970 B.C.

First Samuel 3 is the story of Samuel as a boy about 12 years old, who was living in the Temple under the oversight of Eli, the high priest. Samuel was living in the temple because his godly mother, Hannah, had promised him to the Lord from before birth (see 1 Samuel 1,2). Eli was soon to lose his position and his life because he failed to discipline and control his evil sons. Chapter 3 describes Samuel's first experience of hearing God's voice and the inauguration of an intimate, growing relationship with God, so that it was said, "God let none of Samuel's words fail" (see 1 Samuel 3:19).

Leader's Tip: *Bring the larger group back together and take a few minutes to pray with them. Pray that they will hear God's voice clearly during their study of Acts 8. Then return to your small groups to read the passage and discuss the questions.*

THE SAME GOD WHO SPOKE TO SAMUEL WILL SPEAK TO US TODAY, IF ONLY WE WILL LISTEN

Read Paul's teaching in Acts 8:26-40. Answer the following questions and discuss your responses.

1. What means did Jesus use to speak to Philip (verses 26,29,39,40)?

2. Through what means did God speak to the Ethiopian eunuch (verses 30-35)?

3. What were Philip's and the eunuch's responses to God's Word (verses 27,36-39)?

4. What positive principles about hearing God's voice can we glean from this New Testament example?

5. How does this relate to what we learned from 1 Samuel 3?

SCRIPTURE NOTES

The book of Acts was written by Luke the physician, the author of the Gospel of Luke. Acts should be read as a compendium volume to the Gospel of Luke. Acts 1:8 is an outline of the whole book: "You will receive power when the Holy Spirit comes on you; and you will be my witnesses in Jerusalem, and in all Judea and Samaria and to the ends of the earth."

Acts 8:26-40 records Philip's experience with the Ethiopian eunuch, who held the high position of minister of finance for the Queen of Ethiopia. It is truly remarkable, for it includes an angelic visitation, the Holy Spirit speaking directly to Philip, God speaking to the eunuch through Isaiah 53 and Philip's instruction and the Spirit bodily transporting Philip to Azotus. It is one of many examples in Acts of the dramatic and supernatural spread of the Church throughout the world.

SPECIAL NOTE ON HEARING GOD'S VOICE

When we sense God speaking to us—a form of revelation—or when someone has a word for us—what some call prophecy—we have to evaluate its validity. How are we to test these words to ensure that they are from God and we are not lead astray? Scripture provides a number of safeguards (John Wimber and Kevin Springer, *Power Points*).

1. Personal words should glorify the Word of God, Jesus Christ (see John 16:14).
2. They should conform to the Word of God, the Bible (see Titus 1:9).
3. If a person delivers a word, he or she should be of sound moral character and submitted to the lordship of Jesus (see Matthew 7:15-20).
4. A person delivering prophecies should be willing to have his or her words tested (see 1 Corinthians 14:29-32).

5. Prophetic words should be given in a spirit of love (see James 3:17).
6. Prophecy should not be used to establish doctrine or practice without clear biblical support (see 1 Timothy 6:3).
7. No one should make major decisions based on personal prophetic words alone (see Acts 21:10-14; 1 Corinthians 14:29-32).
8. If a prophetic word predicts future events, it should be fulfilled (see Deuteronomy 18:21,22).
9. Many if not most prophetic words given today are conditional, and as such are invitations, not certainties (see Jeremiah 18:7-10; Jonah 3:4,10).

Remain in your small groups for this section.

Leader's Tip: For the 60-minute session, you will have time to answer only one question.

WORKING IT OUT

Take 10 minutes for 60-minute session
Take 20 minutes for 90-minute session

1. Have you sensed the Holy Spirit speaking to you during this study? What has He been saying?

2. Do you have a desire to be open to the Spirit's leading in ways that He has not used in your life in the past? In what ways?

3. Ask your group to pray that this week God would speak to you the way He spoke to His children in Scripture. Have the group pray specifically for ways that God may want to speak to you and ways you desire Him to speak to you. Come prepared next session to share your experience with the group.

Bring the whole group back together for this section.

Leader's Tip:
Encourage the group to take several days to reflect on and pray daily about this session, asking God to show them what areas of their lives they need to change in light of what they have learned.

LOOKING AHEAD

Take 5 minutes for both sessions

NEXT SESSION: KNOWING GOD

Jesus said, "I do exactly what my Father has commanded me" and He speaks "just what the Father has taught" Him (John 14:31; 8:28). He also stressed to the disciples the importance of hearing and doing what the Father tells them: "Not everyone who says to me, 'Lord, Lord,' will enter the kingdom of heaven, but only he who does the will of my Father who is in heaven" (Matthew 7:21).

If we are going to hear God's voice, we must know who the Father is, how He is related to Jesus and the Holy Spirit and how we experience His blessing. These are the subjects of the next session.

DAILY SCRIPTURE READINGS

Day	Text	Challenge Question
Reflection on This Session		
1	Matthew 17:1-13	The transfiguration is a revelation of God's glory. What did Jesus immediately tell the disciples after the transfiguration (verses 9-13)?
2	John 5:30; 8:26,28; 12:49,50; 14:31	According to these verses, what was the source and power of Jesus' message?
3	Acts 9:1-19	If God came to you as He did to Ananias, would you recognize His voice?
Looking Ahead		
4	John 14:5-31; 16:13,14	According to Jesus, how do we know the Father?
5	Ephesians 1:15-22	What is the "reason" that Paul is referring to (verse 15)? (Hint: see Ephesians 1:1-14.)

In preparation, look at next session's Scripture Notes. Be ready to share your responses to the questions with the rest of the group. Finally, start to memorize the key verse for the next session—John 14:6:

Jesus answered, "I am the way and the truth and the life. No one comes to the Father except through me."

KNOWING GOD

What a long way it is between knowing God and loving him!

Blaise Pascal, French theologian and mathematician, 1623–1662

SESSION FOCUS

One of Jesus' primary purposes for coming to earth was to show us a full revelation of His heavenly Father (see John 1:18) and His highest purposes for us, so that we may intimately know Him.

SESSION KEYS

KEY VERSE (Commit it to memory.)

"Jesus answered, 'I am the way and the truth and the life. No one comes to the Father except through me.'" John 14:6

KEY RESOURCES

J. I. Packer's *Knowing God* (Downer's Grove: InterVarsity Press, 1973); and John Wimber and Kevin Springer's *Power Points* (San Francisco: HarperCollins, 1991), chapters 11,12,15.

SESSION 5 AT A GLANCE

Section	60 Minutes	90 Minutes	What You'll Do
Getting Started	5	5	Pray and Worship
Openers	10	15	Answer and Discuss Questions
Thinking It Through	25	40	Discuss the Meaning of Key Scriptures for Knowing God: John 14:1-31; Ephesians 1:15-22
Working It Out	10	20	Draw Conclusions and Make Life Applications
Looking Ahead	5	5	Preparation for Next Session
Wrapping Up	5	5	Close with Prayer or Song

Break up into groups of three to five people.

OPENERS

Take 10 minutes for 60-minute session
Take 15 minutes for 90-minute session

1. Choose one word from each column below that describes your understanding of your heavenly Father, then tell the group why you chose those terms:

A	B
Accessible	Distant
Compassionate	Demanding
Patient	Impatient
Generous	Niggardly
Affectionate	Unsympathetic
Protective	Cruel
Faithful	Unreliable

2. Return to question 1 above and substitute "Jesus" for "your heavenly Father," then choose one word again from each column. Are they the same words that you chose for "your heavenly Father"? If not, why are they different?

OPTIONAL QUESTION FOR 90-MINUTE SESSION

3. How does your view of God's fatherhood compare with your view of earthly fatherhood?

Bring the whole group back together and the leader should take two to three minutes to introduce this section.

THINKING IT THROUGH

Take 25 minutes for 60-minute session
Take 40 minutes for 90-minute session

While on earth Jesus stressed the intimate relationship between the Father and Himself. He modeled a quality of relationship into which He invited the disciples—and us!—to enter. Jesus was saying, "Look at me and you know the Father. You can know Him in the same way you know Me" (see John 14:6-10).

Consider the conclusion to Jesus' prayer in John 17: "Righteous Father, though the world does not know you, I know you, and they know that you have sent me. I have made you known to them and will continue to make you known in order that the love you have for me may be in them and that I myself may be in them" (verses 25,26). Jesus was praying that we could experience the same quality of the Father's love as He did.

Jesus was in constant communion with His Father and taught the disciples to cultivate the same kind of dependence on and abandonment to the Father. This means several things for us. First, the Father desires fellowship with us. Second, we need not fear rejection when we approach Him in faith. Third, we can pray for the love of the Father to fill our hearts. Finally, there is no request or topic that is too insignificant to talk about with our heavenly Father.

In Matthew 7:21, Jesus said, "Not everyone who says to me, 'Lord, Lord,' will enter the kingdom of heaven, but only he who does the will of my Father who is in heaven." In this incredible statement, Jesus assumes we can know the will of His heavenly Father! And, we are expected to obey as we learn what His will is.

The revelation of the Father is one of the central purposes for which Jesus came. He wants us to know who He is and to know Him intimately. But why is God's fatherhood so important to Jesus? That's the topic of this session.

Now return to your small groups to read the passage and discuss the questions.

JESUS CAME TO REVEAL HIS HEAVENLY FATHER TO US

Read John 14:1-31. Answer the questions that follow and discuss your responses with your group.

1. Why was Jesus so concerned about comforting the disciples in verse 1? (Hint: see John 13:33,36.)

2. What was Jesus' solution for their troubled hearts (John 14:2-4,25-27)?

3. According to Jesus, are there many ways to God (verses 5-8)? (Hint: see Acts 4:12.)

4. Jesus used the word "Father" 23 times in John 14. Why do you think Jesus placed so much emphasis on the Father?

5. What was Jesus' relationship with His Father (verses 10,11,31)?

6. What should our relationship be with our heavenly Father and with His Son (verses 12,20)?

OPTIONAL QUESTIONS FOR 90-MINUTE SESSION

7. According to our heavenly Father, how important is it that we obey Jesus' words (verses 15,21-24)? (Hint: see James 2:14-26.)

8. Based on this entire passage, who should be more influential in our lives—our earthly fathers or our heavenly Father? Why?

SCRIPTURE NOTES

John 14-16 are traditionally called the farewell discourses, followed by the high-priestly prayer in chapter 17. Chapter 14 is a continuation of a table conversation with the disciples that began in chapter 13. In chapter 14 Jesus brings assurance to the disciples, even though He has just told them that He will soon be leaving them. He is taking this opportunity to help them understand the higher purpose in His coming and to call them on to greater faith.

WE WILL NOT RECOGNIZE GOD'S VOICE UNLESS WE KNOW THE HIGHER PURPOSES FOR WHICH HE IS WORKING

Read Paul's prayer in Ephesians 1:15-22. As a group, answer the following questions and discuss your responses.

1. To whom does Paul address his prayers (verse 17)?

2. What is the first thing that Paul wants the Ephesians to receive from the Father (verse 17b)?

3. What is the nature of the power that Paul prays for in verses 18-21?

4. Verse 22 describes Jesus' destiny. How should this future certainty affect how we live today? (Hint: see Ephesians 1:10; Philippians 2:6-11.)

SCRIPTURE NOTES

Paul's letter to the Ephesians connects an intimate relationship with the Father with the fulfillment of God's ultimate purposes on earth for men and women. Written around A.D. 60 to the church in Ephesus (Asia Minor, present-day Turkey), it was probably a circular letter, intended to be read in other churches in the region.

Ephesians 1:15-22 is the first of two prayers found in the letter. (The second is Ephesians 3:14-21.) In both prayers Paul addresses his heavenly Father, praying for wisdom, power and love to fill the believers, so they are able to live fully for God. Jesus and the Holy Spirit are also mentioned prominently in the prayers.

Remain in your small groups for this section.

__Leader's Tip:__ For the 60-minute session, you will have time to answer only one question.

WORKING IT OUT

Take 10 minutes for 60-minute session
Take 20 minutes for 90-minute session

1. What key truth have you learned about your heavenly Father in this study?

2. How has your relationship with your earthly father affected (either positively or negatively) how you relate to your heavenly Father? Pray this week that your heavenly Father would reveal to you His truth and character.

Bring the whole group back together for this section.

Leader's Tip: Encourage the group to take several days to reflect on and pray daily about this session, asking God to show them what areas of their lives they need to change in light of what they have learned.

LOOKING AHEAD

Take 5 minutes for both sessions

NEXT SESSION: INTIMACY WITH THE FATHER

Jesus modeled intimacy with the Father and He called us on to greater intimacy with the Father. For some of us this is frightening, because of bad past experiences. Can I trust Him? Does He truly love me? Is He really committed to me?

Next session we'll look in Scripture at the nature of our heavenly Father and how we can experience a deep, fulfilling relationship with Him that will change our lives.

DAILY SCRIPTURE READINGS

Day	Text	Challenge Question
Reflection on This Session		
1	Ephesians 3:14-21	According to verses 14,15, what should the basis be for our understanding of fatherhood?
2	Nahum 1:2-8	Is there a healthy sense in which we are to fear God?
3	Psalm 103:8-13	What is the key to experiencing God's compassion?
Looking Ahead		
4	Luke 15:11-31	Which of the two sons most deserved the father's love?
5	Hebrews 12:1-13	Why does our heavenly Father discipline us?

In preparation, look at next session's Scripture Notes. Be ready to share your responses to the questions with the rest of the group. Finally, start to memorize the key verses for the next session—Hebrews 12:5,6:

My son, do not make light of the Lord's discipline, and do not lose heart when he rebukes you, because the Lord disciplines those he loves, and he punishes everyone he accepts as a son.

INTIMACY WITH THE FATHER

God soon turns from his wrath, but he never turns from his love.

Charles H. Spurgeon, Baptist preacher,

1834 – 1892

SESSION FOCUS

Our heavenly Father is calling us to experience His love, blessing, forgiveness and discipline, as His obedient sons and daughters.

SESSION KEYS

KEY VERSES (Commit them to memory.)

"My son, do not make light of the Lord's discipline, and do not lose heart when he rebukes you, because the Lord disciplines those he loves, and he punishes everyone he accepts as a son." Hebrews 12:5,6

KEY RESOURCES

Leon Morris's *Jesus Is the Christ* (Grand Rapids: Eerdmans Publishing Co., 1989); and John Wimber and Kevin Springer's *Power Points* (San Francisco: HarperCollins, 1991).

SESSION 6 AT A GLANCE

Section	60 Minutes	90 Minutes	What You'll Do
Getting Started	5	5	Pray and Worship
Openers	10	15	Answer and Discuss Questions
Thinking It Through	25	40	Discuss the Meaning of Key Scriptures for Knowing the Father: Luke 15:11-31; hebrews 12:1-13
Working It Out	10	20	Draw Conclusions and Make Life Applications
Looking Ahead	5	5	Preparation for Next Session
Wrapping Up	5	5	Close with Prayer or Song

*Break up into groups of
three to five people.*

OPENERS

Take 10 minutes for 60-minute session
Take 15 minutes for 90-minute session

1. When as a child you did something wrong and were caught, which of the following best described your reaction:

____ Run and hide

____ Shift the blame to someone else

____ Deny any wrongdoing

____ Only admit the truth when caught red-handed

____ Act ignorant, as if you did not know better

____ Admit wrongdoing and take responsibility

What are you most likely to do now?

2. When you hear the words "discipline" or "punish," what are the first thoughts to come to mind?

OPTIONAL QUESTION FOR 90-MINUTE SESSION

3. One day in heaven the Father is sitting around chatting with Jesus and He begins talking about you. In His proud, fatherly manner, what would He say that would reveal He was pleased with you?

Bring the whole group back together and the leader should take two to three minutes to introduce this section.

THINKING IT THROUGH

Take 25 minutes for 60-minute session
Take 40 minutes for 90-minute session

When you hear the word "father," what is the first image that comes into your mind? Because we live in an imperfect world, mixed in with the biblical images of forgiveness, protection, acceptance and love are often images of betrayal, failure and absence. Unfortunately our thoughts and experiences of earthly fathers can color our images of our heavenly Father.

The best way to overcome past hurts is to experience our heavenly Father's love and acceptance. By experiencing His love we know—really know—in the depths of our beings that we are His children, beloved and accepted by Him. He longs for us to worship Him in intimacy (see John 4:23).

Here are three aspects of the Father's love that, if revealed by the Holy Spirit and taken to heart, can cure the worst cases of heartache and crushed spirits.

✔ First, God's steadfast faithfulness: Even though his son rejected him, the father in Luke 15:20 had not given up hope, but was faithfully watching for the return of his son. Our heavenly Father can always be trusted to do what He has promised (see 1 Thessalonians 5:24).

✔ Second, God's generous blessing: The father showered his very richest blessings on his runaway son when the son returned home (see Luke 15:22,23). He is the source of every good thing and of every perfect gift (see James 1:17).

✔ Third, God's loving discipline: The writer of Hebrews tells us that God's discipline is an undeniable sign that we are children of God and beloved by our heavenly Father (see Hebrews 12:6-8). If we run from God's discipline, we will miss out on "a harvest of righteousness and peace" that He has prepared for us (see Hebrews 12:11).

In this session we'll take a closer look at two attributes of God's love that we experience as we open our hearts to our heavenly Father: His blessing and discipline.

Now return to your small groups to read the passage and discuss the questions.

WHEN WE APPROACH OUR HEAVENLY FATHER HE ENTHUSIASTICALLY SHOWERS US WITH HIS LOVE AND BLESSING

Read the parable of the Father's love in Luke 15:11-32. As a group, answer the following questions and discuss your responses.

1. What was the father willing to risk in letting his son go (verses 12-16)? What does this tell us about the quality of relationship that our heavenly Father wants with us?

2 Describe in detail how the father initially received the unfaithful son when he returned home. Did he receive his son before or after he apologized (verses 20,21)? What does this mean for us when we turn from our sins and return to our heavenly Father?

3. After the initial joy and excitement of the son's return, did the father hold the son's past sins against him (verses 22-24)? What does this tell us about how our heavenly Father looks at our past sins?

4. Compare the father's response to the older brother's sin with his response to the younger brother's sin (verses 28,31).

OPTIONAL QUESTIONS FOR
90-MINUTE SESSION

5. What does the father's response to the unfaithful son's demand tell us about our heavenly Father (verses 11,12)? (Hint: according to Jewish Law, he didn't have to do what he did. See verse 31 and Deuteronomy 21:17.)

6. Compare the older brother's attitude toward his father and younger brother (Luke 15:25-30) with that of the Pharisees in verse 2. What do you think is the source of the older brother's anger?

Scripture Notes provide a simple background to the texts. The leader should review the notes ahead of the study and be prepared to summarize them for the group.

SCRIPTURE NOTES

Luke's Gospel is written by the physician Luke, who was a fellow worker of the apostle Paul. Luke was probably a gentile, well educated and from either Antioch in Syria or Philippi in Macedonia. The Gospel of Luke and the book of Acts are companion volumes, both written to Theophilus. (Some believe that Theophilus was a wealthy Roman official who supported Luke in his ministry.)

Jesus frequently taught in parables. "Parable" comes from the Greek word *parabole*, meaning "a placing beside." Thus, parables teach through illustration or comparison. Jesus drew stories from everyday human life and nature. The Gospels contain about 30 of these stories. Since parables are stories, not every detail in the parable has a spiritual meaning.

Though Luke 15:11-32 is commonly known as the parable of the prodigal son, it is better titled the parable of the Father's love.

OPTIONAL PASSAGE FOR
90-MINUTE SESSION

OUR LOVING FATHER DISCIPLINES HIS SONS AND DAUGHTERS

Read Hebrews 12:1-13. Answer the questions that follow and discuss your responses with your group.

1. In verses 5,6 (which is a quote from the Old Testament, Proverbs 3:11,12), what is the author saying about God's discipline? How can we reconcile this with His love?

2. If we are never disciplined by our heavenly Father, are we true sons and daughters (verses 7,8)?

3. What is the goal and purpose of our heavenly Father's discipline in our lives (verses 9-13)?

4. How does the discipline of a judge differ from the discipline of a father? In which way does God discipline believers?

OPTIONAL QUESTION FOR 90-MINUTE SESSION

5. How do we differentiate an attack from Satan on our lives from God's discipline?

SCRIPTURE NOTES

We do not know who wrote the letter to the Hebrews, though we know he was probably an intellectual Hebrew Christian.

The theme of Hebrews is the absolute supremacy of Christ as the Revealer and Mediator of God's salvation. All of the prophecies and promises of the Old Testament are fulfilled in the New Covenant, which Christ came to fulfill and reveal.

In Hebrews 12 the author addresses the age-old question of why a good God allows bad things (bad, at least, from our perspective) to happen to His children. The answer given here is that God is a loving Father who disciplines us for our good, that we might produce a "harvest of righteousness and peace" (verse 11).

Remain in your small groups for this section.

Leader's Tip: For the 60-minute session, you will have time to answer only one question.

WORKING IT OUT

Take 10 minutes for 60-minute session
Take 20 minutes for 90-minute session

1. What new attributes of the Father did you learn about in this session? How will they affect your relationship with Him?

2. Is there an area of your life in which you have been running away from God? If so, what will you do about it this week?

3. Is there an aspect of your heavenly Father's nature that you have difficulty accepting?

Bring the whole group back together for this section.

Leader's Tip:
Encourage the group to take several days to reflect on and pray daily about this session, asking God to show them what areas of their lives they need to change in light of what they have learned.

LOOKING AHEAD
Take 5 minutes for both sessions

NEXT SESSION: "WHO DO *YOU* SAY I AM?"
During Jesus' life on earth there was much debate among the people about who He is. In Mark 8:27 Jesus asked His disciples, "Who do people say I am?" They said, "John the Baptist," "Elijah," and "one of the prophets" (Mark 8:28).

But then, Jesus looked at His disciples and asked the central question: "Who do you say I am?" (Mark 8:29). He's asking us the same question today. Next session we'll take a close look at the disciples' answer.

DAILY SCRIPTURE READINGS

Day	Text	Challenge Question
Reflection on This Session		
1	John 17:1-26	According to verse 3, what is eternal life?
2	Matthew 6:25-34	Should worry and anxiety be a significant problem for Christians? Why?
3	Ephesians 1:15-23	Why does Paul pray "that you [we] may know him [the glorious Father]" (verse 17)?
Looking Ahead		
4	Philippians 2:3-11	What is the basis for our humility?
5	John 20:24-31	What must we believe to have life in Christ's name (verse 31)?

In preparation, look at next session's Scripture Notes. Be ready to share your responses to the questions with the rest of the group. Finally, start to memorize the key verse for the next session—John 1:18:

No one has ever seen God, but God the One and Only, who is at the Father's side, has made him known.

"WHO DO YOU SAY I AM?"

You should point to the whole man Jesus and say, "That is God."

Martin Luther,
founder of the German Reformation,
1483 – 1546

SESSION FOCUS

Because Jesus is God, we believe He possesses the power to conquer Satan (see Hebrews 2:14), perform miracles that display His Father's glory (see John 11:4,40), conquer death (see John 10:18) and save us from our sin (see 1 Peter 3:18).

SESSION KEYS

KEY VERSE (Commit it to memory.)
"No one has ever seen God, but God the One and Only, who is at the Father's side, has made him known." John 1:18

KEY RESOURCES

John Wimber and Kevin Springer's *Power Points* (San Francisco: HarperCollins, 1991), chapters 16-19.

SESSION 7 AT A GLANCE

Section	60 Minutes	90 Minutes	What You'll Do
Getting Started	5	5	Pray and Worship
Openers	10	15	Answer and Discuss Questions
Thinking It Through	25	40	Discuss the Meaning of Key Scriptures on Chriest's Deity: John 20:24-31; Philippians 2:3-11
Working It Out	10	20	Draw Conclusions and Make Life Applications
Looking Ahead	5	5	Preparation for Next Session
Wrapping Up	5	5	Close with Prayer or Song

Break up into groups of three to five people.

OPENERS

Take 10 minutes for 60-minute session
Take 20 minutes for 90-minute session

1. What is the first thing that comes to mind when you think about who God is?

2. How would you describe God to a child?

OPTIONAL QUESTION FOR 90-MINUTE SESSION

3. What are the most important questions you have about your relationship with Jesus?

Bring the whole group back together and the leader should take two to three minutes to introduce this section.

THINKING IT THROUGH

Take 25 minutes for 60-minute session
Take 40 minutes for 90-minute session

The two most important questions in life are "Who is God?" and "What does He want me to do?" The answer to the second question flows out of the first; as we see and know our Creator, we understand why God has placed us on earth.

So it shouldn't come as a surprise that as Jesus approached the cross, He felt an urgency to clarify His nature to the disciples. The people thought of Jesus in the highest possible human categories, but failed to capture who Jesus was (see Matthew 16:13,14). Jesus pointedly asked His disciples, "Who do you say I am?" (Matthew 16:15). We need to understand who Jesus is in order to know the significance of what He accomplished at the cross.

Anyone can say the words, "Jesus is God." But this isn't the kind of knowledge that Jesus is asking for when He says, "Who do you say I am?" He's asking for a personal commitment, a giving of our hearts to Him as the One-and-only, unique Son of God who has come to forgive sins, give eternal life and fully equip us for ministry in His Kingdom.

Peter's confession (see Matthew 16:16) transcended merely knowing about Jesus, revealing a deep, personal relationship with God. When we have this quality of relationship with God, nothing—not even the "gates [strongholds] of Hades" (Matthew 16:18)—can stop His Church. In Christ, the Church is indestructible!

In this session we'll see how Thomas and Paul responded to Jesus.

Now return to your small groups to read the passage and discuss the questions.

WE ARE BLESSED BY GOD WHEN WE BELIEVE IN JESUS ON THE TESTIMONY OF HIS WORD

Read John 20:24-31. As a group, answer the following questions and discuss your responses.

1. Does Thomas's need to see and touch Jesus' wounds mean he didn't love Jesus? (Hint: see John 11:16; 14:5.) What positive aspect of his character does his skepticism reveal?

2. What does Jesus' appearance and His three statements in John 20:26,27 teach us about faith? (Hint: see John 4:48,53,54; 10:38; 14:11.)

3. Thomas's confession in John 20:28 is one of the high points of confession of faith recorded in the New Testament. How could Thomas change his attitude from doubt to belief so quickly?

4. What important reason did John have for recording the miracles of Jesus (verses 30,31)? What implication does that have for us today?

OPTIONAL QUESTION FOR 90-MINUTE SESSION

5. Why did Jesus consider "blessed" the belief of those who did not personally see His resurrected body (verse 29)? What group of people ("who have not seen and yet have believed") does He have in mind?

Scripture Notes provide a simple background to the texts. The leader should review the notes ahead of the study and be prepared to summarize them for the group.

SCRIPTURE NOTES

The events of John 20:24-31 occur on Easter Sunday and one week later. We don't know why Thomas was not present when Jesus first appeared to the disciples, but it created the circumstances for one of the greatest confessions about Jesus found anywhere in the New Testament ("My Lord and my God!" [verse 28]).

Thomas loved Jesus and was deeply committed to Him. Before the Crucifixion he stated that he was willing to die to follow Jesus (see John 11:16) and later he wanted to know where Jesus was going so he could follow Him (see John 14:5). When Jesus died Thomas was brokenhearted, crushed and defeated. His understanding of the Cross fell short of the Resurrection, so he isolated himself in his grief and missed out on the first post-resurrection appearance.

But Jesus knew his heart. Even in his skepticism, Thomas loved Jesus. When Jesus appeared Thomas was instantly converted to faith. There was a revelation of the

Son of God. Thomas's response, a great confession, was fundamentally a form of worship: "My Lord and my God!"

WE ARE BLESSED BY GOD WHEN WE KNOW WHO JESUS TRULY IS

Read Philippians 2:3-11. Answer the questions that follow and discuss your responses with your group.

1. What was Jesus' identity? (That is, what did Jesus know Himself to be?)

2. What was the basic principle by which Jesus lived His life (verse 8)?

3. How does the model of Jesus' life in these verses differ from the world's values?

4. What impact should Jesus' model of life in these verses have on us as His followers (verses 3-5)?

OPTIONAL QUESTIONS FOR 90-MINUTE SESSION

5. What do you think it means that Jesus emptied Himself, or "made himself nothing" (verse 7)?

6. What is the Father's unalterable plan for Jesus (verses 9-11)?

SCRIPTURE NOTES

Paul wrote the Philippians to thank them for the gift they had sent him and to encourage them by showing them that Jesus is the only source of true joy (see Philippians 4:4). Paul wrote the letter from Rome, where he was in prison. The church in Philippi has the distinction of being the first church established on the European continent.

In Philippians 2:3-11 Paul talks about the basis of unity for all believers: humility. While selfish ambition can ruin a church and undermine a witness for Christ, humility builds God's people and advances the Kingdom. What does true humility look like? Our model is Jesus, after whom we are called to pattern our lives.

Remain in your small groups for this section.

Leader's Tip: For the 60-minute session, you will have time to answer only one question.

WORKING IT OUT

Take 10 minutes for 60-minute session
Take 20 minutes for 90-minute session

1. Are there any areas of the Christian life for which you doubt Jesus? Consider some of the following:
____ Answered prayer
____ The Resurrection
____ Healing
____ Eternal life
____ Forgiveness
____ The authority of Scripture
____ God's fatherly care and provision
____ The leading of the Holy Spirit
____ Other _____

2. What steps can you take this week to act in faith on some area of doubt that you have?

Bring the whole group back together for this section.

Leader's Tip:
Encourage the group to take several days to reflect on and pray daily about this session, asking God to show them what areas of their lives they need to change in light of what they have learned.

LOOKING AHEAD

Take 5 minutes for both sessions

NEXT SESSION: FORGIVENESS IN CHRIST

It took great humility for God to become a man, but that's what Jesus did. "The Word [Jesus] became flesh and made his dwelling among us" (John 1:14).

Though He is God and without sin, Jesus "made himself nothing" and "humbled himself and became obedient to death—even death on a cross" for the forgiveness of our sins and the renewing of intimacy with God (see Philippians 2:7,8). In the next session we'll take a closer look at what motivated God to send His own Son to the cross and why we can have forgiveness through the cross.

DAILY SCRIPTURE READINGS

Day	Text	Challenge Question
Reflection on This Session		
1	Mark 14:53-65	Why did the high priest tear his clothes (verse 63)?
2	John 1:1-18	What does this passage claim about Jesus' nature (verses 1,14,18)?
3	Mark 2:1-12	Why did some of the teachers of the law think Jesus was blaspheming?
Looking Ahead		
4	Luke 7:36-50	Does Jesus' treatment of the sinful woman mean He doesn't take sin seriously?
5	Hebrews 10:10-18	How long is the offering of Jesus on the cross good for?

In preparation, look at next session's Scripture Notes. Be ready to share your responses to the questions with the rest of the group. Finally, start to memorize the key verse for the next session—Romans 5:8:

But God demonstrates his own love for us in this: While we were still sinners, Christ died for us.

FORGIVENESS IN CHRIST

He breaks the power of canceled sin,
He sets the prisoner free
His blood can make the foulest clean;
His blood availed for me.

Charles Wesley,
British preacher and hymn writer,
1707 – 1788

SESSION FOCUS

Only God's free act of forgiveness can restore our relationships with Him. Jesus' work on the cross is that free act of forgiveness, which needs to be experienced personally by faith.

SESSION KEYS

KEY VERSE (Commit it to memory.)
"But God demonstrates his own love for us in this: While we were still sinners, Christ died for us." Romans 5:8

KEY RESOURCES
Michael Green's *The Empty Cross of Jesus* (Downer's Grove: InterVarsity, 1984); Martyn Lloyd-Jones's *The Cross* (Wheaton: Good News Publications, 1986); and John Wimber and Kevin Springer's *Power Points* (San Francisco: HarperCollins, 1991), chapters 20-22.

SESSION 8 AT A GLANCE

Section	60 Minutes	90 Minutes	What You'll Do
Getting Started	5	5	Pray and Worship
Openers	10	15	Answer and Discuss Questions
Thinking It Through	25	40	Discuss the Meaning of Key Scriptures on Forgiveness: Luke 7:36-50; Hebrews 10:10-18
Working It Out	10	20	Draw Conclusions and Make Life Applications
Looking Ahead	5	5	Preparation for Next Session
Wrapping Up	5	5	Close with Prayer or Song

Break up into groups of three to five people.

OPENERS

Take 10 minutes for 60-minute session
Take 15 minutes for 90-minute session

1. C. S. Lewis once wrote, "Everyone says forgiveness is a lovely idea, until they have something to forgive." Do you agree with this statement? In your own life, have you found this to be true? Explain.

2. Has a friend or relative ever asked you for forgiveness for a sin they committed against you? If so, how did it make you feel?

OPTIONAL QUESTION FOR 90-MINUTE SESSION

3. What would be the most difficult thing to forgive someone for?

Bring the whole group back together and the leader should take two to three minutes to introduce this section.

THINKING IT THROUGH

Take 25 minutes for 60-minute session
Take 40 minutes for 90-minute session

A study about the gift of God's forgiveness assumes that men and women are sinners in need of God's grace. Many of us, however, are tempted to fool ourselves by:

• Shifting the blame, like Adam and Eve in Genesis 3.

• Repressing our guilt by trying to cover it up and deny its existence. We may blame others or relentlessly avoid facing up to our failures.

• Regretting our mistakes. We say, "I'm sorry," and then seek to justify our actions, failing to acknowledge the seriousness of our sin and to take responsibility for it.

• Feeling remorse. We say, "I wish I'd never done that"—then promise we'll never do it again. We feel sorry about what we did, or at least about being caught in our wrongdoing.

All of these responses fall far short of recognizing our sins: "If we claim to be without sin, we deceive ourselves and the truth is not in us" (1 John 1:8). Only through heartfelt, honest recognition of sin can we prepare ourselves to receive God's forgiveness. As Corrie ten Boom once said, "The blood of Jesus never cleansed an excuse."

In the remainder of this session we'll explore the nature of God's forgiveness and how we can receive it.

Now return to your small groups to read the passage and discuss the questions.

JESUS HAS THE POWER AND AUTHORITY TO FORGIVE SINNERS, BECAUSE HE IS GOD

Read Luke 7:36-50. As a group, answer the questions that follow and discuss your responses.

1. What three things did the woman do when she saw Jesus? What do you think motivated her (verses 37,38,47)?

2 What was Simon's response to the woman and what does it tell you about him (verse 39)?

3. What is the main point of the parable in verses 40-43? (Hint: see verse 47.) What does this say to us today?

4. What was the basis for Jesus forgiving the woman's sin (verses 47-50)? In addition to forgiveness, what else did Jesus say the woman received (verse 50)?

OPTIONAL QUESTION FOR 90-MINUTE SESSION

5. Why do you think Simon, a religious leader, invited Jesus to dinner (verses 36,40,44-47)?

Scripture Notes provide a simple background to the texts. The leader should review the notes ahead of the study and be prepared to summarize them for the group.

SCRIPTURE NOTES

Luke 7:36-50 describes a "sinful" woman (probably a prostitute) barging into a meal at Simon the Pharisee's home. Most likely the meal was held in an open courtyard at Simon's home, in which all kinds of people were free to come in and listen to the conversation. The guests would lie around a low table, with their feet extending away from the table.

Normally when guests came into a home they were offered three courtesies as signs of respect. First, their feet were washed, for they wore sandals and walked dusty roads. Second, they received a kiss of peace, as a form of greeting and honor. Third, a drop of aromatic oil or a touch of sweet-smelling incense was placed on their heads. Simon offered none of these, indicating a lack of respect for Jesus.

The "sinner woman," however, went far beyond normal courtesy, wetting Jesus' feet with tears of repentance, kissing His feet and anointing Him with costly perfume (also see John 12:3).

Jesus frequently taught in parables (see Luke 7:40-43). In this parable of two men owing a moneylender money, Jesus is contrasting two attitudes of heart and mind toward sin and forgiveness. Simon had no consciousness of sin and thus did not realize his need for forgiveness. The woman, however, was quite aware of her sin and saw in Jesus the source of forgiveness and true love.

OPTIONAL PASSAGE FOR 90-MINUTE SESSION

JESUS CAN FORGIVE US BECAUSE HE UNIQUELY TAKES OUR PLACE (HE IS OUR SUBSTITUTE), ENDURING GOD'S WRATH FOR OUR SINS

Read Hebrews 10:10-18. Answer the following questions and discuss your responses with your group.

1. How are the sacrifices of the high priest contrasted with Jesus' death on the cross (verses 10-12)?

2. How long is the offering of Jesus on the cross good for (verse 14)?

3. What does the writer say about the sins that are covered by the once-and-for-all sacrifice of Jesus (verses 17,18)?

Scripture Notes

Hebrews 10:10-18 is in the context of a contrast between the high priest and his offerings and the one-time, good-for-ever sacrifice of the High Priest Jesus offering up His life for us as a substitute. Because Jesus is fully man, He could die (see Hebrews 2:14). Because Jesus is fully God, He could die for us, redeeming sinful men and women and restoring God's original intention that we might rule the earth under Him (see Hebrews 1:3).

Remain in your small groups for this section.

Leader's Tip: For the 60-minute session, you will have time to answer only one question.

Working It Out

Take 10 minutes for 60-minute session
Take 20 minutes for 90-minute session

1. Are there any sins that you have committed for which you still find it difficult to receive forgiveness from God? Without going into detail, ask the group to pray for you, that you might believe and receive forgiveness in Christ.

2. Are their any sins that have been committed against you that you still find it difficult to forgive the other person? Ask the group to pray that you can see the person who sinned against you as Christ sees him or her—a sinner in need of grace. Then on your own pray and forgive him or her on the basis of the blood of Jesus.

Bring the whole group back together for this section.

Leader's Tip:
Encourage the group to take several days to reflect on and pray daily about this session, asking God to show them what areas of their lives they need to change in light of what they have learned.

LOOKING AHEAD

Take 5 minutes for both sessions

NEXT SESSION: TAKING UP OUR CROSS

Jesus' death on the cross secures forgiveness and eternal life for us. But it also has life-changing implications for how we live our lives.

When we come "under the blood of Jesus," we become like Jesus—taking on His cause, character and values. And there is no greater value than sacrifice: "I urge you, brothers," Paul wrote, "in view of God's mercy, to offer your bodies as living sacrifices, holy and pleasing to God" (Romans 12:1). Next session we'll look at how sacrifice is at the heart of true life change.

DAILY SCRIPTURE READINGS

Day	Text	Challenge Question
Reflection on This Session		
1	Matthew 9:1-8	Did Jesus refer to His humanity or deity when He healed the paralytic?
2	Matthew 18:21-35	What is the relationship between our ability to receive forgiveness from God and to forgive those who have sinned against us?
3	Romans 5:1-2	What motivated God to send His only Son to the cross to die for you and me (verse 8)?
Looking Ahead		
4	Matthew 16:21-28	Why did Jesus address Peter as an adversary ("Satan") in verse 23?
5	Matthew 13:44-46	How much must we be willing to sacrifice for the kingdom of heaven?

In preparation, look at next session's Scripture Notes. Be ready to share your responses to the questions with the rest of the group. Finally, start to memorize the key verse for the next session—Matthew 16:24:

> [Jesus said] "If anyone would come after me, he must deny himself and take up his cross and follow me."

TAKING UP OUR CROSS

He is no fool who gives what he cannot keep to gain what he cannot lose.

Jim Elliot,
twentieth-century missionary and martyr

SESSION FOCUS

Jesus Christ died on the cross for us; therefore no sacrifice is too great for us to make for Him. Sacrifice for Jesus releases His power.

SESSION KEYS

KEY VERSE (Commit it to memory.)

[Jesus said] "If anyone would come after me, he must deny himself and take up his cross and follow me." Matthew 16:24

KEY RESOURCES

Elisabeth Elliot's *Through Gates of Splendor* (Wheaton: Tyndale House Publishers, 1986) and John Wimber and Kevin Springer's *Power Points* (San Francisco: HarperCollins, 1991), chapter 23.

SESSION 9 AT A GLANCE

Section	60 Minutes	90 Minutes	What You'll Do
Getting Started	5	5	Pray and Worship
Openers	10	15	Answer and Discuss Questions
Thinking It Through	25	40	Discuss the Meaning of Key Scriptures on Personal Sacrifice: Matthew 16:21-28; 13:44-46
Working It Out	10	20	Draw Conclusions and Make Life Applications
Looking Ahead	5	5	Preparation for Next Session
Wrapping Up	5	5	Close with Prayer or Song

Break up into groups of three to five people.

OPENERS

Take 10 minutes for 60-minute session
Take 15 minutes for 90-minute session

1. Frederick P. Wood once said, "The only life that counts is the life that costs." Do you agree with this statement? Have you ever sacrificed something (money, career, relationship) that cost you greatly? Explain.

2. When you hear the word "sacrifice," are your first thoughts primarily positive or negative? Explain.

OPTIONAL QUESTIONS FOR 90-MINUTE SESSION

3. Anything worth living for is worth dying for. What (or who) would you be willing to die for? What are you living for today?

4. Have you ever made a large sacrifice for a person or a cause that later proved to be a disappointment? How does it affect your willingness to sacrifice today?

Bring the whole group back together and the leader should take two to three minutes to introduce this section.

THINKING IT THROUGH

Take 25 minutes for 60-minute session
Take 40 minutes for 90-minute session

Once two American businessmen who were visiting Korea were amused to see a young farmer in a field, harnessed to a plow and being directed by his father. When they described the scene to a missionary friend, they were told that the farmers had sold their only ox and given the money to their church.

The businessmen were amazed. "What a stupendous sacrifice!" one exclaimed.

But the missionary responded, "They did not feel that way about it. They counted it a great joy that they had an ox to give to the Lord's work."

Testimonies like the Korean farmers' remind us that sometimes God calls us to quite literally fulfill Paul's words in Romans 12:1: "I urge you, brothers, in view of God's mercy, to offer your bodies as living sacrifices, holy and pleasing to God."

It's easy, though, to get caught up in the external actions of our sacrifice, forgetting that it is acceptable to God only when we are motivated by an attitude of obedience and devotion to the Lord: "Does the Lord delight in burnt offerings and sacrifices as much as in obeying the voice of the Lord? To obey is better than sacrifice and to heed is better than the fat of rams" (1 Samuel 15:22).

Jesus used two powerful symbols to teach us about sacrificial living: the cross and a pearl of great price. The first teaches us the basis for sacrificial living, the latter teaches us the focus and cost.

Now return to your small groups to read the passage and discuss the questions.

WE ARE ABLE TO SACRIFICE OUR LIVES FOR GOD BECAUSE HE SACRIFICED HIS SON FOR US

Read Matthew 16:21-28. Answer the questions that follow and discuss your responses with your group.

1. Why did Jesus rebuke Peter so harshly in verse 23? (Hint: see verses 21,22.) Why did Jesus call Peter "Satan"?

2. How is our taking up of a cross different from Jesus' taking up the cross? How is it similar (verse 24)?

3. What do Jesus' seeming paradoxes concerning life in verse 25 say to us about how we spend our lives?

4. According to Jesus, what future event brings eternal significance to our present actions and attitudes (verses 26,27)?

OPTIONAL QUESTION FOR 90-MINUTE SESSION

5. What was Jesus referring to when He said in verse 28, "some who are standing here will not taste death before they see the Son of Man coming in his kingdom"? (Hint: see Matthew 17:1-13; John 14:15-21; Acts 1:1-11; 2:1-5.)

Scripture Notes provide a simple background to the texts. The leader should review the notes ahead of the study and be prepared to summarize them for the group.

SCRIPTURE NOTES

Matthew 16:21-28 marked the beginning of a new emphasis in Jesus' ministry. Instead of teaching on the Kingdom of God in parables (see below), He began to concentrate on teaching the disciples about the meaning of His coming death and resurrection.

Peter's inability to accept Christ's coming death indicates he did not understand what it meant for Christ to be the "Anointed One"—the Messiah (see Matthew

16:16). What is remarkable about Christ's sharp rebuke of Peter is that it came only moments after Jesus blessed Peter, acknowledged the divine revelation in his words and said Peter was to build Jesus' church on Peter's confession of Christ (see Matthew 16:17). Jesus had to convince the disciples that the cross was the only way to the Father. And if He had to be crucified, they would also need to take up their crosses daily.

"Satan" literally means adversary. When Peter wanted to stand between Jesus and the cross, he was trying to prevent the greatest triumph in human history, the day that Satan, sin and death would be forever defeated. Only Satan himself could inspire Peter's thinking, so Jesus rebuked him in the most powerful way possible.

THE KINGDOM OF GOD IS OF SUCH GREAT VALUE THAT WE SHOULD BE WILLING TO GIVE UP EVERYTHING FOR IT

Read Matthew 13:44-46. As a group, answer the following questions and discuss your responses.

Jesus frequently taught in parables. "Parable" comes from the Greek word *parabole*, meaning "a placing beside." Parables teach through illustration or comparison. Jesus drew stories from everyday human life and from nature to teach about His reign. Parables teach one central truth, so we cannot find symbolic meaning in every detail.

1. What was the cost in the two parables? The gain?

2. Why did the man and the merchant willingly and joyfully pay such a great cost?

3. Were the words used to describe their actions passive or active? What does this say about the focus of our lives?

SCRIPTURE NOTES

The good news Jesus proclaimed was the gospel of the Kingdom of God. The word "kingdom" does not emphasize so much a realm as a reign; the "right of God to rule," that He has all authority and power. (Matthew, writing to Jews, uses the more familiar term "Kingdom of heaven" instead of Kingdom of God.) The book of Mark records Jesus preaching, "The time has come," as He begins His public ministry. "The kingdom of God is near. Repent and believe the good news!" (Mark 1:15).

The heart of Jesus' message was both the proclamation and demonstration of God's action—"The kingdom...is near"—and the demand for a response from all who heard—"Repent and believe."

Jesus was proclaiming nothing less than the hope of our salvation: God has come to redeem and bless us and establish His reign over all the earth. This salvation was summed up in the idea that the "Kingdom of God" was close—in fact, Jesus came to usher it in. Every miraculous act of Jesus had a purpose: to confront people with His message that in Him the Kingdom had come and that they had to decide to accept or reject it.

Matthew 13:44-46, the parables of the hidden treasure and the pearl, is found in a series of parables on the Kingdom of God (13:1-52). In it Jesus teaches one of the most significant truths we can ever understand about the Kingdom: we must invest everything for the Kingdom, because of its incomparable value.

Remain in your small groups for this section.

Leader's Tip: For the 60-minute session, you will only have time to answer one question.

WORKING IT OUT

Take 10 minutes for 60-minute session
Take 20 minutes for 90-minute session

The man and the merchant sacrificed (invested) all that they had—willingly, with joy—because they realized the incomparable value of the treasure and the pearl. It all made perfect sense to them to sell all.

1. Does it make sense to you to follow Jesus without compromise? Is your focus more on your problem, circumstance, or weakness; or is your focus on the incomparable Christ, the reigning King?

2. Ask yourself, "Is Jesus speaking to me today about sacrificing something for the Kingdom of God?" (See the following list.) What steps will you take this week to do it?
___ Potential marriage partner
___ Close friendship
___ Career
___ Education
___ Money
___ Popularity
___ Material possession (e.g. house, car, clothes)
___ Entertainment
___ Sport
___ Hobby
___ Time
___ Other _____

Bring the whole group
back together for this
section.

LOOKING AHEAD

Take 5 minutes for both sessions

Leader's Tip:
Encourage the group to
take several days to
reflect on and pray daily
about this session, asking
God to show them what
areas of their lives they
need to change in light of
what they have learned.

NEXT SESSION: POWER FOR VICTORIOUS LIVING

Paul writes, "For it is by grace you have been saved, through faith—and this is not from yourselves, it is a gift of God" (Ephesians 2:8). For Paul, good works flow out of a relationship with Jesus. But how do we live by grace—by love we haven't earned? The secret to successful Christian living is learning to depend on the Holy Spirit to lead, teach, empower and equip us to fulfill God's work. In the next session we'll explore our relationship with the Holy Spirit.

DAILY SCRIPTURE READINGS

Day	Text	Challenge Question
Reflection on This Session		
1	Luke 21:1-4	What does the widow's example tell you about financial giving?
2	John 15:12-15	Has the Lord ever asked you to lay down something for His sake?
3	Acts 7:57—8:3	What did Stephen gain from his sacrifice?
Looking Ahead		
4	Galatians 5:13-26	What is the key to no longer gratifying the desires of our sinful nature?
5	Ephesians 5:15-21	Summarize what it means to be filled with the Spirit.

In preparation, look at next session's Scripture Notes. Be ready to share your responses to the questions with the rest of the group. Finally, start to memorize the key verse for the next session—John 16:13:

[Jesus said] "But when he, the Spirit of truth, comes, he will guide you into all truth."

POWER FOR VICTORIOUS LIVING

If we wish to be men and women who can live victoriously, we need this two-sided gift God has offered us: first, the work of the Son of God for us; second, the work of the Spirit of God in us.

Billy Graham, evangelist

SESSION FOCUS

Of the three Persons of the Trinity, the Holy Spirit is actually the closest to us, dwelling personally in our hearts (see John 14:17) and empowering us to live above our sinful natures.

SESSION KEYS

KEY VERSE (Commit it to memory.)
[Jesus said] "But when he, the Spirit of truth, comes, he will guide you into all truth." John 16:13

KEY RESOURCES
Billy Graham's *The Holy Spirit* (Dallas: Word, 1988); Michael Green's *I Believe in the Holy Spirit* (Grand Rapids: Eerdmans Publishing Co., 1989); and John Wimber and Kevin Springer's *Power Points* (San Francisco: HarperCollins, 1991), chapters 24-27.

SESSION 10 AT A GLANCE

Section	60 Minutes	90 Minutes	What You'll Do
Getting Started	5	5	Pray and Worship
Openers	10	15	Answer and Discuss Questions
Thinking It Through	25	40	Discuss the Meaning of Key Scriptures on the Holy Spirit: Galatians 5:13-26; Ephesians 5:15-21
Working It Out	10	20	Draw Conclusions and Make Life Applications
Looking Ahead	5	5	Preparation for Next Session
Wrapping Up	5	5	Close with Prayer or Song

Break up into groups of three to five people.

OPENERS

Take 10 minutes for 60-minute session
Take 15 minutes for 90-minute session

1. If you had unlimited power to change one thing about yourself, what would it be?

2. Have you ever had an experience in which, at the time, you were sure you were going to die? What happened? What explanation do you have for your survival?

OPTIONAL QUESTION FOR 90-MINUTE SESSION

3. How would you describe the Holy Spirit to a child?

Bring the whole group back together and the leader should take two to three minutes to introduce this section.

THINKING IT THROUGH

Take 25 minutes for 60-minute session
Take 40 minutes for 90-minute session

In John 7:37,38, Jesus said, "If anyone is thirsty, let him come to me and drink. Whoever believes in me, as the Scripture has said, streams of living water will flow from within him." John then comments, "By this he [Jesus] meant the Spirit, whom those who believed in him were later to receive" (John 7:39). Jesus is calling us to a zealous thirst for God, one which He promises to satisfy through His Spirit.

Later, in John 16:7, Jesus told the disciples, "It is for your good that I am going away. Unless I go away, the Counselor [the Spirit] will not come to you; but if I go, I will send him to you." Jesus was so confident in the work of the Holy Spirit that He claimed it was *for our good* that He go to be with the Father!

In His last post-resurrection appearance, just prior to the ascension, Jesus instructed the disciples to "Wait for the gift my Father promised....You will be baptized with the Holy Spirit" in order to be witnesses "to the ends of the earth" (Acts 1:4,5,8). True to Jesus' word, the Holy Spirit filled the Church on Pentecost and 3,000 Jews from all over the world were converted after hearing Peter preach the gospel.

How does the Holy Spirit come to us today? And what do we have to do to experience His life-transforming presence in our lives? That's the topic of this session.

Now return to your small groups to read the passage and discuss the questions.

THE HOLY SPIRIT IS SENT TO BUILD CHRISTIAN CHARACTER IN US, SO WE ARE NO LONGER ENSLAVED TO OUR SINFUL NATURES

Read Galatians 5:13-26. As a group, answer the questions that follow and discuss your responses.

1. According to Paul, what does true personal freedom look like (verses 13-15)? How does this differ from the world's definition of personal freedom? (Hint: see Romans 8:1-4.)

2. How do you know whether you are being led by the Holy Spirit or by your sinful nature (Galatians 5:16-18)? (Hint: keep reading!)

3. In verse 21, does Paul mean that if we commit one of the previously mentioned acts we will not inherit the Kingdom of God? (Hint: see 1 John 3:4-10.) How, then, are we to understand this verse?

4. If those in Christ "have crucified the sinful nature" (Galatians 5:24), why do we keep on sinning? (Hint: see Romans 7:21-25.)

OPTIONAL QUESTIONS FOR
90-MINUTE SESSION

5. In Galatians 5:23, what does Paul mean when he says, "Against such things there is no law"?

6. In verse 25, what does Paul mean when he says, "Since we live by the Spirit, let us keep in step with the Spirit"? (Hint: see John 10:4.)

Scripture Notes provide a simple background to the texts. The leader should review the notes ahead of the study and be prepared to summarize them for the group.

SCRIPTURE NOTES

Paul wrote his letter to the Galatians to address problems created by Judaizers, Jewish Christians who insisted that many Old Testament ceremonial practices were still required in the New Testament church. They even taught that Gentile converts needed to be circumcised.

Because Paul opposed them, they argued that he was not an authentic apostle, that he was watering down the gospel by failing to add legal requirements to it. Their personal attack on him was a way of undermining his message.

Paul's response was forceful and direct. By adding legal requirements to the gospel, Paul wrote, the Judaizers perverted Christ's work on the cross. Paul carefully lays a foundation of grace—that we are justified by Jesus' completed work on the cross and not by our works—then explodes at the beginning of chapter 5: "It is for freedom that Christ has set us free. Stand firm, then and do not let yourselves be burdened again by a yoke of slavery."

In 5:13-26 Paul anticipates the critics' question: If we are no longer under the Law, how do we live out the Christian life. His answer? We have the Holy Spirit: He indwells us, empowers us, leads us and produces good fruit (mature character) in us.

WE ARE COMMANDED TO COOPERATE WITH THE WORK OF THE HOLY SPIRIT IN LIVING THE CHRISTIAN LIFE

Read Ephesians 5:15-21. Answer the following questions and discuss your responses with your group.

1. What does Paul command us to do in verse 18? How do we do it?

2. According to verses 19,20, what does a person who is filled with the Spirit look like?

3. Contrast the results of being filled with the Holy Spirit with the results of being filled with wine.

SCRIPTURE NOTES

Paul's letter to the Ephesians was written around A.D. 60, while he was in prison in Rome. It was probably a circular letter, intended to be read in other churches in the region of Asia Minor, now Turkey.

In 5:15-22, Paul says, in effect, you've got to be filled with something—so make it the Holy Spirit. He contrasts being filled with wine with being filled with God's Spirit. The world gets happy on wine; Christians are happy when they are full of the Spirit. What are the results? Paul outlines three here, though certainly there are more: mouths filled with spiritual songs; hearts overflowing with thankfulness to God; minds bent on honoring brothers and sisters.

*Remain in your small
groups for this section.*

Leader's Tip: *For the
60-minute session, you
will have time to answer
only one question.*

WORKING IT OUT

Take 10 minutes for 60-minute session
Take 20 minutes for 90-minute session

1. The Bible teaches that it is God's will for us to be filled with the Holy Spirit (Ephesians 5:18). Have you ever experienced the filling of the Holy Spirit? If you have not, or if you are not sure if you have, pray along with other members of the group for His filling. Paul says "the Lord is the Spirit" (2 Corinthians 3:17) and, as such, we can call on Him. Here's a suggested prayer:

"Holy Spirit, I invite you to fill my life with your presence. Please fill every part of my body and soul with your love and power, so I can in your strength fulfill Your Word. I submit myself to You and to Your leading for my life."

If you are holding back an area of your life from God, He's calling on you to yield it to Him and be filled with His Spirit.

*Bring the whole group
back together for this
section.*

LOOKING AHEAD

Take 5 minutes for both sessions

Leader's Tip:
*Encourage the group to
take several days to
reflect on and pray daily
about this session, asking
God to show them what
areas of their lives they
need to change in light of
what they have learned.*

NEXT SESSION: GIFTS FOR GENEROUS GIVING

Spiritual gifts are "given for the common good" of the Church (see 1 Corinthians 12:7). The gifts have nothing to do with personal ambition or career orientation.

They are not given to build individual reputations, to warrant superior positions in the local church, or to demonstrate spiritual advancement. They are not trophies, but tools—tools for touching, blessing and serving others.

Next session we'll look at how God wants to release the gifts in us.

DAILY SCRIPTURE READINGS

Day	Text	Challenge Question
Reflection on This Session		
1	John 7:37-39	What does Jesus promise us if we believe in Him?
2	John 16:5-16	Summarize the work of the Spirit in the world.
3	Acts 1:1-9; 2:1-4	According to Acts 1:8, for what purpose was the Spirit sent to help us fulfill?
Looking Ahead		
4	1 Corinthians 12:1-11	For what purpose are spiritual gifts given to the Church?
5	1 Corinthians 12:12—13:3	When are we baptized in the Holy Spirit (1 Corinthians 12:13)?

In preparation, look at next session's Scripture Notes. Be ready to share your responses to the questions with the rest of the group. Finally, start to memorize the key verse for the next session—1 Corinthians 14:1:

Follow the way of love and eagerly desire spiritual gifts, especially the gift of prophecy.

GIFTS FOR GENEROUS GIVING

All the gifts of this Church stem from one source—God. What Paul says in the twelfth chapter of his First Epistle to the Corinthians is still true today!

Ignatius of Loyola, in Spiritual Exercises,
1525

SESSION FOCUS

God is at work in us, manifesting Himself through gifts of the Spirit for the common good of the Church. Love allows the gifts to flourish among us.

SESSION KEYS

KEY VERSE (Commit it to memory.)
"Follow the way of love and eagerly desire spiritual gifts, especially the gift of prophecy." 1 Corinthians 14:1

KEY RESOURCES

Billy Graham's *The Holy Spirit* (Dallas: Word, 1988); Michael Green's *I Believe in the Holy Spirit* (Grand Rapids: Eerdmans Publishing Co., 1989); and John Wimber and Kevin Springer's *Power Points* (San Francisco: HarperCollins, 1991), chapters 28-29.

SESSION 11 AT A GLANCE

Section	60 Minutes	90 Minutes	What You'll Do
Getting Started	5	5	Pray and Worship
Openers	10	15	Answer and Discuss Questions
Thinking It Through	25	40	Discuss the Meaning of Key Scriptures on the Gifts of the Spirit: 1 Corinthians 12:1–13:3;
Working It Out	10	20	Draw Conclusions and Make Life Applications
Looking Ahead	5	5	Preparation for Next Session
Wrapping Up	5	5	Close with Prayer or Song

Break up into groups of three to five people.

OPENERS

Take 10 minutes for 60-minute session
Take 15 minutes for 90-minute session

1. Back in the fifth century, Saint Augustine wrote, "It is a simple fact that there is no lack of miracles even in our day. And the God who works the miracles we read in the Scripture uses any means and manner he chooses." Do you think his statement is equally valid for today? Explain your answer.

2. Is there a spiritual gift that you would like to experience? Why?

Bring the whole group back together and the leader should take two to three minutes to introduce this section.

THINKING IT THROUGH

Take 25 minutes for 60-minute session
Take 40 minutes for 90-minute session

On August 15, 1750, John Wesley wrote in his journal: "The grand reason why the miraculous gifts were so soon withdrawn, was not only that faith and holiness were wellnigh lost, but that dry, formal, orthodox men began even then to ridicule whatever gifts they had not themselves and to decry them all as either madness or imposture."

Controversy has always surrounded spiritual gifts. When the Holy Spirit came on Pentecost and many spoke in tongues, there were witnesses who accused them of drunkenness. When the "apostles performed many miraculous signs and wonders," the people became fearful (see Acts 5:11-13). Nevertheless, many were healed and delivered of evil spirits—and "more and more men and women believed in the Lord and were added to their number" (Acts 5:14).

It didn't help that some Christians abused the gifts. In his first letter to the Corinthians, Paul addresses—among other issues—the misuse of the gifts. First Corinthians 12 and 14—the two most prominent passages found in the New Testament on the gifts—are sandwiched around Paul's memorable words on love in chapter 13. The context is clear: without love, the gifts are of no value.

Now return to your small groups to read the passage and discuss the questions.

SPIRITUAL GIFTS ARE GIVEN FOR THE COMMON GOOD OF THE BODY OF CHRIST

Read 1 Corinthians 12:1-11. As a group, answer the following questions and discuss your responses.

1. In verses 1-3, Paul contrasts Christianity with mute idols. How is the God of the Bible different from mute idols? How does this affect our relationship with Him?

2. What is the key point that Paul makes in verses 4-6?

3. What does verse 7 teach us about our motivation as we pursue and exercise spiritual gifts?

4. Do you believe verses 8-10 contain a complete list of the spiritual gifts? (Hint: see Romans 12:3-8; 1 Corinthians 12:28; Ephesians 4:11-13.)

OPTIONAL QUESTION FOR 90-MINUTE SESSION

5. According to 1 Corinthians 12:11, who should expect to receive spiritual gifts? Who determines which gift(s) we will receive?

SPIRITUAL GIFTS ARE GIVEN TO BUILD UP THE BODY OF CHRIST IN UNITY

Read 1 Corinthians 12:12—13:3. Answer the following questions and discuss your responses with your group.

1. In 1 Corinthians 12:12,13, Paul compares the Church to the human body—implying that Jesus is now present on earth in us. How important, then, are you to Christ's witness? Explain.

2. Based on verses 14-16 of chapter 12, how important is your participation in the Church? What happens if you withdraw?

3. 1 Corinthians 12:17-20 implies that we do not all have the same function. (Verse 28 speaks of God appointing regular functions related to the gifts.) Do you know what your function is in the Body?

4. What is the "most excellent way" in 1 Corinthians 12:31b? (Hint: see 1 Corinthians 13:1-3.)

OPTIONAL QUESTIONS FOR 90-MINUTE SESSION

5. According to verses 21-26 of chapter 12, what is the key to maintaining unity in the Body?

6. Do you "eagerly desire the greater gifts" (1 Corinthians 12:31a)? What are the greater gifts?

Scripture Notes provide a simple background to the texts. The leader should review the notes ahead of the study and be prepared to summarize them for the group.

SCRIPTURE NOTES

The first letter to the Corinthian church was written by Paul around A.D. 55, toward the end of his three-year stay in Ephesus (1 Corinthians 16:5-9; Acts 20:31). Corinth, with a population of over 650,000, was a leading Greek city.

Paul was writing the church to address several significant problems:

• Factions were ripping the church apart (see 1 Corinthians 1:11);

• Sexual immorality was polluting the Body (see 1 Corinthians 5,6);

• They were resolving legal conflicts among themselves in pagan courts (see 1 Corinthians 6:1-8);

• They were abusing the Lord's Supper (see 1 Corinthians 11:17-34);

• They were tolerating false teaching about the Resurrection (see 1 Corinthians 15);

• They needed instruction regarding the poor believers in Jerusalem (see 1 Corinthians 16:1-4).

And, of course, their immaturity and disunity showed in the way they handled spiritual gifts (see 1 Corinthians 11:17—14:40).

Chapter 12 begins, "Now about spiritual gifts"—of which Paul said they had no lack (1 Corinthians 1:7). A spiritual gift is a gift of grace from God, a manifestation of the Holy Spirit that builds up the Body of Christ and witnesses to Christ's presence in the world. There can be no division in the Church based on the gifts; they are given to build the Body in love and unity.

Paul contrasts a God who speaks and manifests His

presence in the Body of Christ with mute idols. No where does he indicate the gifts are limited only to the first century and no where does he discourage the use of gifts because of their potential for abuse. Instead, he says they are a key blessing and of the keys to building the Body in love and unity. Indeed, in 1 Corinthians 12:31 he says we should "eagerly desire the greater gifts"—a call to seek God for His gifts in order to glorify Him and bless our brothers and sisters!

Remain in your small groups for this section.

Leader's Tip: For the 60-minute session, you will have time to answer only one question.

WORKING IT OUT

Take 10 minutes for 60-minute session
Take 20 minutes for 90-minute session

Have you ever asked God to manifest His gifts in you? If not, seek Him this week for spiritual gifts. If you feel comfortable, ask one or two members of the group to pray that the Holy Spirit would manifest new spiritual gifts in your life.

Bring the whole group back together for this section.

Leader's Tip: Encourage the group to take several days to reflect on and pray daily about this session, asking God to show them what areas of their lives they need to change in light of what they have learned.

LOOKING AHEAD

Take 5 minutes for both sessions

NEXT SESSION: GIVING AWAY OUR FAITH

Jesus' mission was to make His Father known to men and women (see John 14:6) and we too have been commissioned to spread the same good news. In John 15:26-27 Jesus teaches us, "When the Counselor comes, whom I will send to you from the Father, the Spirit of truth who goes out from the Father, he will testify about me. And you also must testify, for you have been with me from the beginning."

Michael Green writes, "The joy of Christian living atrophies if it is not shared." In the next session we'll look at the Great Commission and explore how to give our faith away to others.

DAILY SCRIPTURE READINGS

Day	Text	Challenge Question
Reflection on This Session		
1	Romans 12:3-8	How does this list of gifts differ from the one found in 1 Corinthians 12:8-11?
2	Ephesians 4:1-13	How is the list in verses 11-13 different from the lists in 1 Corinthians 12:8-11 and Romans 12:6-8?
3	Hebrews 2:1-4	Can you think of any spiritual gifts that confirmed the gospel in the New Testament? (Hint: see Acts 2:1-4.)
Looking Ahead		
4	Matthew 9:35-38	Which of the following does Jesus say there is a lack of: people to evangelize, or Christians to spread the gospel?
5	Matthew 28:16-20	In verses 19,20, Jesus commands us to do three things in the Great Commission. Can you summarize them?

In preparation, look at next session's Scripture Notes. Be ready to share your responses to the questions with the rest of the group. Finally, start to memorize the key verse for the next session—1 Peter 3:15:

Always be prepared to give an answer to everyone who asks you to give the reason for the hope that you have. But do this with gentleness and respect.

GIVING AWAY OUR FAITH

I look upon all the world as my parish; thus far I mean, that, in whatever part of it I am, I judge it meet, right and my bounden duty to declare unto all that are willing to hear, the glad tidings of salvation.

John Wesley, founder of the Methodist Movement, 1703 -91

SESSION FOCUS

Jesus commissioned us to present the good news of the cross in the power of the Holy Spirit, so that men and women will put their trust in God through Him and experience eternal life.

SESSION KEYS

KEY VERSE (Commit it to memory.)
"Always be prepared to give an answer to everyone who asks you to give the reason for the hope that you have. But do this with gentleness and respect." 1 Peter 3:15

KEY RESOURCES
Paul Little's *How to Give Away Your Faith* (Downer's Grove: InterVarsity Press, 1988); Rebecca Manley Pippert's *Out of the Saltshaker* (Downer's Grove: InterVarsity Press, 1979); John Wimber and Kevin Springer's *Power Evangelism, Revised Edition* (San Francisco: HarperCollins, 1991); and John Wimber and Kevin Springer's *Power Points* (San Francisco: HarperCollins, 1991), chapters 30-31.

SESSION 12 AT A GLANCE

Section	60 Minutes	90 Minutes	What You'll Do
Getting Started	5	5	Pray and Worship
Openers	10	15	Answer and Discuss Questions
Thinking It Through	25	40	Discuss the Meaning of Key Scriptures on Evangelism: Matthew 9:35—10:8; 28:16-20; Mark 4:26-29
Working It Out	10	20	Draw Conclusions and Make Life Applications
Looking Ahead	5	5	Preparation for Next Session
Wrapping Up	5	5	Close with Prayer or Song

Break up into groups of three to five people.

OPENERS

Take 10 minutes for 60-minute session
Take 15 minutes for 90-minute session

1. How did you become a Christian?

2. How would you respond if someone asked you why you became a Christian?

3. Do you struggle with one of the following barriers to sharing your faith with others? Explain your answer.

- Fears of being ridiculed and rejected; of appearing fanatical or weird; of turning people off.
- Feeling I'm imposing my ideas on others.
- I'm not convinced in my heart that personal evangelism is my job.
- I don't believe that I will do any good, because I easily forget the source of power in my witness.
- I don't know what to say.

*Bring the whole group
back together and the
leader should take two to
three minutes to intro-
duce this section.*

THINKING IT THROUGH

Take 25 minutes for 60-minute session
Take 40 minutes for 90-minute session

A recent study indicates that 86 percent of all Christians came to a saving faith in Jesus through the testimony of a friend or relative (Larry Gilbert, *TEAM Evangelism*. Church Growth Institute, Virginia). Advertising, pastoral visits and organized evangelistic outreaches accounted for only 14 percent!

We shouldn't be surprised about these statistics, because this was exactly how Jesus planned it. In Matthew 28:19,20 He commissioned the disciples to "Therefore go and make disciples of all nations...teaching them to obey everything I have commanded you." In this, the Great Commission, God called every individual believer to reproduce what God has done for and in them in others—to spread the good news that Jesus has died on the cross to forgive sins and give eternal life.

The Great Commission would be an overwhelming task were it not for two important sources of power. First, the gospel itself has intrinsic power, the power to persuade and save. Paul writes, "I am not ashamed of the gospel, because it is the power of God for the salvation of everyone who believes" (Romans 1:16). The message of the Cross penetrates hearts, overcomes fears, defeats unbelief!

The second source of power is the Holy Spirit. In His last post-resurrection appearance to the disciples, Jesus instructed them to "wait for the gift my Father promised" [the Holy Spirit] in order to "receive power" and "be my witnesses in Jerusalem, and in all Judea and Samaria, and the ends of the earth" (Acts 1:4,5,8). On Pentecost the Spirit came and 3,000 were added to the Church! So our message has power and we are empowered messengers.

God has arranged it so that we are the only Bible that some people will ever hear. If we proclaim the message of the Cross in the power of the Spirit, Jesus will do the rest. Paul wrote, "You show that you are a letter from Christ, the result of our ministry, written not with ink but with the Spirit of the living God, not on tablets of stone but on tablets of human hearts" (2 Corinthians 3:3). Spiritual growth is important not only for our own benefit, but for the benefit of others who will be changed through the message we carry.

Now return to your small groups to read the passage and discuss the questions.

JESUS TAUGHT THERE ARE MANY PEOPLE WAITING TO HEAR THE MESSAGE OF SALVATION; ALL THAT'S NEEDED ARE FAITH MESSENGERS

Read Matthew 9:35—10:8. As a group, answer the following questions and discuss your responses.

1. In verse 35 of chapter 9, Jesus combines two kinds of activity. What are they and what does this teach you about how you should approach evangelism today?

2. Why did Jesus have compassion for the crowd in verse 36? Do you feel that kind of compassion for the lost?

3. What is the harvest Jesus is speaking of in verse 37? (Hint: see John 4:34-38.)

4. Who are the workers in Matthew 9:38 and what work do you think Jesus is calling them to do?

5. In Matthew 10:7,8, Jesus instructs the disciples, commanding two kinds of activities. What are they and who is their model?

IN THE GREAT COMMISSION JESUS COMMANDED US TO MAKE DISCIPLES OF ALL THE NATIONS

Read Matthew 28:16-20. Answer the questions that follow and discuss your responses with your group.

1. What were the circumstances surrounding the timing and location of the Great Commission (verse 16)? Why are these circumstances significant and what do they tell you about being called to ministry?

2. What does the disciples' reaction to Jesus in verse 17 tell you about them? Is this encouraging or discouraging?

3. Why did Jesus preface the Great Commission with verse 18? What significance does it hold for what follows (verse 20b)?

4. There are at least three primary mandates to the Great Commission (verses 19,20a). Can you summarize them?

Scripture Notes provide a simple background to the texts. The leader should review the notes ahead of the study and be prepared to summarize them for the group.

SCRIPTURE NOTES

Matthew 9:35 is a three-fold summary of Jesus' ministry. First, He preached the good news (gospel) of the Kingdom of God. By this He meant that God's rule had come to earth and He was going to overcome evil and redeem men and women. Second, He taught from God's Word, the source of all wisdom and truth for godly living. Finally, He demonstrated the gospel through healing and signs and wonders. The combination of proclamation and demonstration of the gospel produced a remarkable evangelistic harvest.

Matthew 9:36 reveals God's heart for the lost. He has compassion for them. Love motivated the Father to sacrifice His Son (see John 3:16) and compassion motivates the Son to offer eternal life to the lost. Understanding and experiencing Jesus' heart for the lost is prerequisite to being an effective harvester of souls (see Matthew 9:37,38).

Matthew 28:16-20 contain Jesus' last recorded words in the gospel, leaving a lasting impression that we have been saved from eternal judgment for a purpose here on earth. Every Christian, from the youngest to the oldest, is called to make disciples. There is an urgency to the task, for in the age to come there will be no redemption, only eternal joy and rejoicing as we live in the presence of our heavenly Father. But for a time—short when compared to eternity—we are commissioned to go throughout the world and preach the good news of the Cross.

OPTIONAL PASSAGE FOR
90-MINUTE SESSION

THE POWER OF THE GOSPEL IS IN THE SEED—THE GOSPEL ITSELF; WE SPREAD THE GOOD NEWS AND GOD CAUSES IT TO GROW

Read Mark 4:26-29. Answer the following questions and discuss your responses.

1. Based on verse 26, should you worry about sharing the gospel with too many people? Why?

2. What do verses 27 and 28 tell you about evaluating the effectiveness of your evangelistic efforts? Who is ultimately responsible for any evangelistic harvest?

3. What does the soil symbolize in verse 28? (Hint: see Matthew 4:13-20.)

SCRIPTURE NOTES

Mark's Gospel was written by John Mark, who was an associate of Peter. His mother, Mary, was a prominent person in the New Testament church (see Acts 12:12). She was Barnabas's aunt (see Colossians 4:10). He deserted Paul and Barnabas during their first missionary journey (see Acts 15:37,38), which led to Paul and Barnabas going different ways. By the end of Paul's life they were reunited (see 2 Timothy 4:11).

Mark 4:26-29 is part of a series of Jesus' parables on the Kingdom of God. Unlike many of His other parables, this one is not repeated in the other Gospels. Clearly the point to this parable is that the seed itself has power, implying the gospel message contains power. We are the messengers of a powerful, life-changing message.

Remain in your small groups for this section.

WORKING IT OUT

Take 10 minutes for 60-minute session
Take 20 minutes for 90-minute session

1. Do you feel the sense of compassion and urgency for the lost that Jesus modeled? If not, ask one or two others in the group to pray that the Holy Spirit would create in you a new heart and urgency to share the gospel.

2. Do you wish you had more opportunities to share your faith with others? If you do, ask that one or two others would pray that between now and the next session God would arrange a "divine appointment" with a nonbeliever in which you could share the gospel. Come to the next session prepared to describe your evangelistic experience.

Bring the whole group back together for this section.

LOOKING AHEAD

Take 5 minutes for both sessions

Leader's Tip:
Encourage the group to take several days to reflect on and pray daily about this session, asking God to show them what areas of their lives they need to change in light of what they have learned.

NEXT SESSION: PREPARING FOR SPIRITUAL WARFARE

Ephesians 6:12 says, "For our struggle is not against flesh and blood, but against the rulers, against the authorities, against the powers of this dark world and against the spiritual forces of evil in the heavenly realms." This verse applies to every aspect of the Christian life, which means we should expect spiritual conflict, because we've been placed here for a while longer to overcome the works of Satan and set people free.

In the next session—the last of this series—we'll look at the nature of spiritual warfare and how God has equipped us to defeat Satan.

DAILY SCRIPTURE READINGS

Day	Text	Challenge Question
Reflection on This Session		
1	Luke 19:1-10	How did Jesus know Zacchaeus's name?
2	John 16:1-15	Summarize the work of the Spirit in the world.
3	Acts 1:1-9; 2:1-4	According to Acts 1:8, for what purpose was the Spirit sent to help us fulfill?
Looking Ahead		
4	2 Corinthians 10:3-5	How do we demolish the world's strongholds (verse 5)?
5	Ephesians 6:10-20	Who is our ultimate enemy?

In preparation, look at next session's Scripture Notes. Be ready to share your responses to the questions with the rest of the group. Finally, start to memorize the key verse for the next session—Ephesians 6:12:

For our struggle is not against flesh and blood, but against the rulers, against the authorities, against the powers of this dark world and against the spiritual forces of evil in the heavenly realms.

PREPARING FOR SPIRITUAL WARFARE

𝒯he bread that you store up belongs
to the hungry; the cloak that lies on
your chest belongs to the naked
and the gold that you have hidden in
the ground belongs to the poor.

St. Basil,
missionary and theologian,
330–79

Session Focus

A primary purpose of Jesus' coming is to destroy the work of the devil (see 1 John 3:8). God has equipped us with defensive armor and offensive weapons to demolish satanic strongholds.

Session Keys

Key Verse (Commit it to memory.)

"For our struggle is not against flesh and blood, but against the rulers, against the authorities, against the powers of this dark world and against the spiritual forces of evil in the heavenly realms." Ephesians 6:12

Key Resources

John Wimber and Kevin Springer's *Power Points* (San Francisco: HarperCollins, 1991), chapters 32-34.

SESSION 13 AT A GLANCE

Section	60 Minutes	90 Minutes	What You'll Do
Getting Started	5	5	Pray and Worship
Openers	10	15	Answer and Discuss Questions
Thinking It Through	25	40	Discuss the Meaning of Key Scriptures on Spiritual Warfare: 2 Corinthians 10:3-5; Ephesians 6:1-20; Luke 4:16-21
Working It Out	10	20	Draw Conclusions and Make Life Applications
Wrapping Up	5	5	Summary and Prayer

Break up into groups of three to five people.

OPENERS

Take 10 minutes for 60-minute session
Take 15 minutes for 90-minute session

1. When you hear the term "spiritual warfare," what comes to your mind?

2. Have you ever been in a situation in which you sensed there was supernatural spiritual warfare going on around you? Describe it to the group.

Bring the whole group back together and the leader should take two to three minutes to introduce this section.

THINKING IT THROUGH

Take 25 minutes for 60-minute session
Take 40 minutes for 90-minute session

In Matthew 10:34 Jesus made a puzzling statement: "Do not suppose that I have come to bring peace to the earth. I did not come to bring peace, but a sword." The Prince of Peace (see Isaiah 9:6) then described how His presence would create intense family conflict and division and how we had to love Him more than our families.

How are we to understand these words, coming from the same person who said, "Peace I leave with you; my peace I give you" (John 14:27a)?

The answer is found in the nature of the peace that Jesus offers us. Continuing in John 14:27, He says, "I do not give to you as the world gives. Do not let your hearts be troubled and do not be afraid." The peace that Jesus gives is different from what the world promises. He gives us our redemption on the cross—forgiveness of sins, reconciliation with His Father, assurance of eternal life.

But it comes with a high price tag to us while we remain on earth: "All men will hate you because of me, but he who stands firm to the end will be saved" (Matthew 10:22). The world will hate and reject us, because it is under the control of Satan. The moment we transfer our citizenship to the Kingdom of God through faith in Christ, we come into immediate conflict with everything the world stands for. We are thrust into a battle in which there is no neutral ground.

Satan wants us back. There's nothing too rotten, too low, that he won't resort to in order to defeat us. He wars on our bodies, minds and emotions.

But Jesus doesn't send us into a battle ill-equipped. He has already done everything at the cross to keep us secure and to assure our victory. In this, the last session in *The Way to Maturity* study, we'll look at the nature of spiritual battle and how we are equipped to stand firm for the gospel.

Now return to your small groups to read the passage and discuss the questions.

THE KEY BATTLEGROUND IS THE HEARTS AND MINDS OF MEN AND WOMEN

Read 2 Corinthians 10:3-5. Answer the questions that follow and discuss your responses with your group.

1. What does God's word say about the weapons we fight with (verse 4)?

2. What are the "strongholds" that Paul refers to in verse 4? (Hint: see verse 5.)

3. Where do the primary spiritual battles take place? (Hint: see Colossians 2:8.)

4. How do we demolish false arguments and pretensions and "take captive every thought"? (Hint: see Ephesians 6:19; Colossians 4:3,4.)

SCRIPTURE NOTES

Paul wrote the second letter to the Corinthians in A.D. 55, shortly before winter, from Macedonia (see 2 Corinthians 2:13; 7:5). He had written his first Corinthian letter in the spring of the same year (see Acts 20:31; 1 Corinthians 16:5-9). Corinth, with a population of over 650,000, was a leading Greek city.

In the first letter Paul addressed such problems as divisions, sexual immorality, legal conflicts in pagan courts, abuse of the Lord's Supper, false teaching and abuse of spiritual gifts. In the second letter Paul refuted false teachers who said his teaching could not be trusted and who claimed he was a false apostle. They even brought his character into question. (They accused him of financial impropriety.)

Second Corinthians 10:3-5 is part of a larger defense of Paul's ministry. He vigorously defended himself, because he knew if his character and calling were destroyed, his message of the Cross would be undermined. Paul is up for a good fight, but he never forgets the true nature of the battle. He used weapons different from the world to demolish strongholds of evil arguments and pretensions that oppose truth.

THE WORD OF GOD GIVES US SPECIFIC INSTRUCTIONS ABOUT HOW TO FIGHT THE WAR AGAINST UNSEEN FORCES IN HEAVENLY REALMS

Read Ephesians 6:10-20. As a group, answer the following questions and discuss your responses.

1. What are the "authorities," "powers of this dark world," and "spiritual forces of evil in the heavenly realms" that Paul refers to verse 12?

2. What is the primary purpose for the "armor of God" (verse 13)? What are the results for you personally if you opt out of wearing the armor and fighting the war Paul is talking about?

3. In verses 14-17a there are five pieces of defensive armor. Circle all five. Which one(s) is (are) the most important for you right now? Why?

4. Verses 15,17b-20 describe four offensive weapons, two of which have counterparts in Roman armor. What are the four offensive weapons?

Scripture Notes provide a
simple background to the
texts. The leader should
review the notes ahead of
the study and be pre-
pared to summarize
them for the group.

SCRIPTURE NOTES

Ephesians 6:10-20 comes within the larger context of teaching on unity in the Body of Christ. The key to showing the love of the Father in Christ to the world is our unity and that can only be maintained if our relationships are in good order. With that in mind, Paul then addresses the true cause of all disunity: spiritual battles taking place in the heavenly realms. When we view our brothers and sisters as our enemies we fail to understand that there is a powerful unseen world surrounding us.

Ephesians 6:10-20 provides specific instructions about how to fight the battle. Most of the armor is defensive, indicating we must take the enemy seriously for he can inflict great hurt on us. But this doesn't imply our position is purely defensive. We take territory—the hearts and minds of men and women—as we wield God's word, pray and preach the gospel with boldness and clarity.

OPTIONAL PASSAGE FOR
90-MINUTE SESSION

Read Luke 4:16-21. Answer the questions that follow and discuss your responses.

1. According to verse 18, to whom was Jesus sent by God to preach the good news?

2. Who are "the poor" (verse 18b)?

3. In what sense was the Scripture fulfilled in Jesus' reading (verse 21)?

4. Do you believe Jesus' ministry 2,000 years ago has any relation to ours today? (Hint: see John 10:21.)

SCRIPTURE NOTES

Luke 4:16-21 is a summary of Jesus' earliest recorded sermons, leading to the beginning of His public ministry. Jesus' custom of regular worship created the environment for His commentary from Isaiah 61:1,2.

At that time the service was broken down into three parts. First, the people worshiped God. Next, seven people were selected to read from the Scriptures, first in Hebrew (which they didn't understand), then it was translated into Aramaic or Greek (which they could understand). Finally, distinguished members or visitors were invited by the synagogue's president—they didn't have formal ministers—to teach. A discussion would follow.

It was at this seminal time in His ministry that Jesus chose to emphasize ministry to the poor, prisoners, blind and oppressed. In the Old Testament the "year of the Lord's favor" was the year of Jubilee, in which debts were to be remitted, slaves freed and land redistributed. Jesus announced the impending establishment of an eternal Jubilee.

Remain in your small groups for this section.

Leader's Tip: *For the 60-minute session, you will have time to answer only one question.*

WORKING IT OUT

Take 10 minutes for 60-minute session
Take 20 minutes for 90-minute session

1. Are you currently involved in a situation or relationship in which you sense God telling you to ask for courage and boldness to speak His truth? Share it with the group and receive prayer.

2. Do you believe you are doing enough to minister to the poor, prisoners, blind and oppressed where you live? Are there any opportunities to do so in your church or geographic area? Ask God to show you where you can get involved.

Bring the whole group back together.

Leader's Tip:
Encourage the group to take several days to reflect on and pray daily about this session, asking God to show them what areas of their lives they need to change in light of what they have learned.

DAILY SCRIPTURE READINGS

Day	Text	Challenge Question
	**Reflection on This Session**	
1	Daniel 10:12—11:1	What part did Daniel play in defeating the prince of the Persian kingdom (verse 10:13)? Did he even know of the existence of the evil principality?
2	2 Kings 6:8-23	What does this passage tell you about the unseen world?
3	Colossians 2:9-15	In our battle with "the powers and authorities," where was the key battle fought? Who won?

POWER POINTS

A KEY RESOURCE FOR THE SERIOUS DISCIPLE

John Wimber and Kevin Springer write in greater depth about all of the topics in this study in their book, *Power Points*. You may purchase it at your local Christian bookstore, or order it from:

Vineyard Ministries International
P.O. Box 68025
Anaheim, CA 92817

Make your check out to VMI for $15.95 and be sure to include your full name, complete return address and the words *Power Points*.

Or, Call 1-800-852-VINE and purchase on your
VISA or MasterCard.

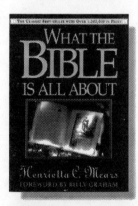
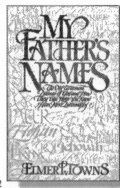
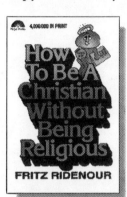

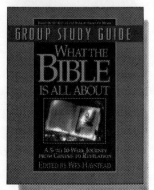
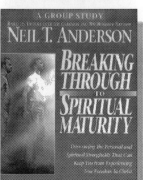